Second Treatise of Government

Crofts Classics

GENERAL EDITOR

Samuel H. Beer, *Harvard University*

JOHN LOCKE

An Essay Concerning the True Original, Extent and End of Civil Government

Second Treatise of Government

EDITED BY

Richard H. Cox

STATE UNIVERSITY OF NEW YORK AT BUFFALO

Harlan Davidson, Inc.
Wheeling, Illinois 60090-6000

 Address inquiries to Harlan Davidson, Inc., 773 Glenn Avenue, Wheeling, Illinois, 60090-6000.

Visit us on the World Wide Web at www.harlandavidson.com.

Library of Congress Cataloging-in-Publication Data

Locke, John, 1632–1704.
Second treatise of government.

Bibiliography: p.
1. Political science—Early works to 1700. 2. Liberty. 3. Toleration.
I. Cox, Richard Howard, 1925–. II. Title.
JC153.L85 1982 320.1 85-2516
AACR2

ISBN 0-88295-124-6

ISBN 0-88295-125-4 (pbk.)
ISBN 978-0-88295-125-6

Manufactured in the United States of America
08 07 06 05 16 17 18 19 VP

contents

introduction[1]

John Locke's precursor, Francis Bacon, once said, "Some books are to be read only in parts; others to be read, but not curiously; and some few to be read wholly, and with diligence and attention."[2] Locke's *An Essay Concerning the True Original, Extent and End of Civil Government*—the second of his *Two Treatises of Government*—is the third kind of book, for it is a work of political philosophy. Such works contain the concentrated thought of philosophic minds, focussed on basic questions concerning the nature of political things: What is justice? What is property? What is the best form of government? What is law? What is the purpose of political society? The serious reader of a work of political philosophy seeks, in effect, to ascend to the summit of thought concerning these questions by

[1]To "introduce" a work of political philosophy is, to some extent, to "interpret" it. *Introduce* comes from a Latin root, *intro-ducere*, which means "to lead into" or "to lead within." Similarly, *interpret* comes from a Latin root, *interpretari*, which means "to explain" or "to expound," with a more remote root in older words that mean "to spread abroad between others." Drawing on these etymological senses, I conceive of my Introduction as seeking to lead the reader "within" Locke's *Second Treatise* by "explaining" certain of its most important features.

On the problem of interpreting, see Michael Platt, "Interpretation," *Interpretation*, 5, no. 1 (Summer 1975): 109–130.

[2]Francis Bacon, "Of Studies," in *Essays or Counsels, Civil and Moral* (1625).

rethinking the thoughts of the philosopher. The following remarks on Locke's *Second Treatise of Government* offer guidelines for that ascent.

Part I is a sketch of Locke's life and times. It is meant to set Locke's writings within their historical and intellectual framework in order to help the present-day reader grasp his purpose and meaning. Part II is an overview of Locke's five main writings. It argues that Locke's *Second Treatise* is best understood as part of a grand intellectual design for the fundamental restructuring of society and thus of human life. Part III is a compressed analysis of the structure and content of the *Two Treatises.* This analysis permits the reader from the outset to see the main lines of Locke's argument and thus prepares the way for an intensive reading of the *Second Treatise.* Part IV discusses the interpretation and the significance of Locke's political teaching.

I. Locke's Life and Times

John Locke was born in 1632 and died in 1704.[3] He thus lived through some of the most tumultuous events in English history: the Civil War between Royalists and Roundheads (1642–1649), the establishment and collapse of Oliver Cromwell's "Commonwealth" (1649–1660), the Restoration of the Monarchy (1660), and the continuing religious-political controversies that were largely resolved in the Glorious Revolution (1688–1689) and the Act of Settlement of the Crown (1701).

Locke was born to Puritan parents of modest means. He was educated at Westminster School (London) and Christ Church College (Oxford), largely supported by scholarships. At Oxford he followed the traditional curriculum in natural and moral philosophy. He also became interested in the new experimental study of nature and in medicine, but he pursued both interests informally.

[3]A concise biography of Locke may be found in the *English Dictionary of National Biography*. In what follows I am much indebted to Maurice Cranston's *John Locke* (London: Longmans, 1957).

In the summer of 1666 Locke met Lord Ashley, later to become the first earl of Shaftesbury and one of the principal Whig opponents of the restored monarchy. It was a fateful meeting: Locke soon became not only personal physician to Ashley but also a political advisor. Late in 1666, by order of the Court and perhaps with the help of Ashley, Locke was appointed as a physician at Christ Church over the objection of the Oxford medical faculty.

As the conflict between the Whigs and Charles II intensified, so did the danger for Ashley and his physician-advisor. Thus, in 1677 Ashley was sent to prison in the Tower for a year. In 1679 the college librarian at Christ Church became a secret, unofficial spy for the Court, keeping it informed of Locke's doings and whereabouts. Again in 1681 Ashley was thrown into the Tower and released only because the grand jury, loaded with Whigs, refused to indict him. Upon his release, Ashley actively sought to raise a Whig rebellion. But when that failed, he fled to the political refuge of Holland late in 1682, where he died early in 1683.

Locke now became ever more fearful for his own safety. He too sought asylum in Holland, arriving there in September 1683. But he was not forgotten by his enemies in England: In 1684 the King ordered him expelled from his position at Christ Church and placed his name on a list of alleged "conspirators," which was presented to the Dutch States General with the demand that the named persons be extradited to England for trial. Locke then went into hiding. He used aliases and concealed his whereabouts from all but close friends. And even when he came out of hiding in 1686, after James II had come to the throne, he took pains to conceal the location of his residence and was very cautious in his correspondence. Finally, early in 1689 he returned to England, but only when it appeared reasonably safe to do so because of the imminent transfer of the crown to Protestant William and Mary of Holland.

From 1689 to 1700, when failing health greatly restricted his activities, Locke divided his time between writing and public service. He took an active part in weighty controversies over public policies, particularly those having to do with various aspects of trade. He published two works (one in 1691 and one in 1695) that discuss the problems of the legal regulation of interest rates and the state of the coinage in England.[4] He sought to show that the workings of natural laws of productivity and exchange cannot be overcome by unwise civil laws and that to seek to do so is to ensure serious harm to the economy, hence to the common interest in a thriving, powerful political society. One important consequence of his arguments was the recoinage that eventually had a beneficial effect on English trade. As for public service, in 1696 William III appointed Locke a commissioner of the newly founded Board of Trade. Locke served in that post until 1700, much occupied with very practical matters such as the linen trade in Ireland, the choice of administrators in the colonies, and policy toward paupers. His abilities and influence were recognized again by William III in 1698, for he was personally offered a position by the King—apparently the important post of embassy secretary in Paris. Locke declined because of his poor health and because he wished to devote more time to his studies and writings. But he remained a notable public figure until very near the end of his life.

Thus Locke was no mere reclusive philosopher. And yet in retrospect his role in the great political controversies of his time proves to have been far less important than was his role in the great intellectual controversy that also was going on. That controversy—the most fundamental in the intellectual history of the West—is sometimes known as "the quarrel between the ancients and the moderns." In 1704, the year Locke died, Jonathan Swift (1667–1745) published a remarkably acute satire on the quarrel in *The Battle of the Books.* And in 1726 he published a much more intricate satire, his most famous work, *Gulliver's Travels.* A brief survey of one aspect of the opposition between ancients and moderns that Swift satirized will help to set Locke's writings in their proper philosophical framework.

The basic opposition was between the ancients' essentially "contemplative" and the moderns' essentially "manipulative" understanding of the ultimate nature and purpose of

[4]*Some Considerations of the Consequences of the Lowering of Interest; Further Considerations Concerning Raising the Value of Money.*

human knowledge. The ancients spoke of the vehicle of human knowledge as the *psyche* or soul; they conceived of the highest activity of the soul as *theoria*—active wondering and gazing at the cosmos and its various parts; and they concluded that the true object of *theoria* is simply knowledge for the sake of knowledge. In more concrete terms, the *theoria* of classical physics, for example, consists of observation and reflection concerning the nature of motion and rest. Knowledge of that nature is an end in itself, complete and perfect. In contrast, the moderns increasingly spoke of the vehicle of human knowledge as the mind; they conceived of the highest activity of the mind as the discovery of methods by which the mind may penetrate nature's secrets by developing a dialectic between theory and experiment; and they concluded that the true object of that dialectic is the acquisition of human power over natural processes. Knowledge is for the sake of human power. Again in more concrete terms, the theory of modern physics is a progressive interchange between hypotheses concerning the laws of physical processes and experiments, which themselves often require the very extensive and intensive manipulation of physical things. Thus, the moderns thought, the knowledge *of* things in nature is contingent upon and revealed by human power *over* nature and the object of knowledge is the making of new things that serve human desires. Francis Bacon, whom Swift perceived as one of the most formidable of the moderns, summarized this aspect of the modern conception of human knowledge in a remarkable phrase: He argued that the object of knowledge is "the conquest of nature for the relief of man's estate."

Today it is difficult to grasp, let alone give much credence to, the teaching of the ancients, so thorough has been the acceptance of the teaching of the moderns. But for the purpose of studying Locke's works, it must constantly be kept in mind that when he lived and wrote the issue between ancients and moderns was still very much undecided. As a matter of fact, when Locke wrote his five most important works—*A Letter Concerning Toleration, Two Treatises of Government, An Essay Concerning Human Understanding, The Reasonableness of Christianity,* and *Some Thoughts Concerning Education*—political, religious, and university authorities joined forces to restrain and even to prevent the articulation of unorthodox doctrines, including the "modern" principles. First of all, the government licensed and censored written works. Locke's *Two Treatises,* for example, was licensed by the government in the fall of 1689; without that license, it could not have been published. Second, a vigorous polemic was waged against the works of the most obvious advocates of the modern principles, as well as against those who were suspected of harboring sympathies for that camp. For example, a raging invective bespattered the main political works of Thomas Hobbes (*Of the Citizen,* 1642, and *Leviathan,* 1651) when they were published. Hobbes, an open advocate of the modern principles, was variously described as "The Monster of Malmesbury," a defamer of human nature in his account of man in the state of nature, and even an outright atheist, in spite of the elaborate exegeses of biblical passages Hobbes presented as proofs that his teachings were consonant with the biblical ones. And toward the end of the century Locke's own *Reasonableness of Christianity*—published anonymously like most of his works—was subjected to the harsh charge that its teaching was merely a thinly disguised form of Hobbism.

A third kind of repression of unorthodox doctrines occurred when public authorities sometimes subjected alleged miscreants to the full force of criminal law, such as to statutes which forbade blasphemy or sedition. A young man of eighteen was publicly hanged at Edinburgh in 1696. His crime: public denial of the doctrine of the trinity, a blasphemy he was alleged to have learned in part from reading Hobbes' writings. Earlier Algernon Sidney, a Whig leader, was beheaded in the Tower of London in 1683. His crime: the "treasonous" assertion of the superiority of republican over monarchical government, an assertion he was alleged to have made in his unpublished work, *Discourses on Government,* a writing clearly influenced by Machiavelli's *Discourses on Livy.*

In sum, when Locke wrote and published, harassment, calumny, and even outright persecution were serious possibilities and sometimes painful realities for those who dared to teach unorthodox principles of morals, religion, or government too openly. With this in mind, let us look at Locke's personal circumstances and his conduct with respect to the publication of his first three major works.

Locke completed the *Letter, Treatises,* and *Essay Concerning Human Understanding* while a hunted exile in Holland. In 1689 he published the *Letter* anonymously in a Latin version in Holland, and the *Treatises,* also anonymously but in London. In 1690 he published the *Essay* in London; it alone of all three works carried his name on the title page. Thus, within a year's time, as we *now* know, but hardly anyone in the world *then* knew except Locke himself, Locke published two works on religion and politics and one on the abstruse question of the workings of the human mind. He never publicly acknowledged either the *Letter* or the *Treatises* during the remaining fourteen years of his life. He did so in fact only when he suspected death was near and then only in a codicil to his will. On the other hand, he acknowledged the *Essay* from the outset and publicly defended it against all critics. Apparently Locke felt free to publish openly and to defend in his own name a work on human understanding but not those on religion and politics.

To see more exactly why, let us look closely at the *Letter.* On the title page of the original Latin edition are some mysterious letters. Maurice Cranston has shown that they are the first letters of a Latin phrase that means, in part: written by one who is a "friend" of peace and a "hater" of persecution.[5] Above all, Locke must have had religious persecution by political authority in mind, for the *Letter* itself contains the essence of the doctrine of separation of church and state. We now take that doctrine nearly for granted as true or proper, especially in the United States, but when Locke published his *Letter,* it was bold and unorthodox. That is shown not only by Locke's great reluctance to acknowledge the *Letter* as his own but even more so by the stream of scathing criticism directed against it in the pamphlet literature of the times. Locke published three rebuttals to that criticism, always anonymously, and in these he admitted the unorthodox character of the

[5]Cranston, *op. cit.*, p. 320.

Letter's doctrine. Given the circumstances his policy of anonymity was not paranoia but merely prudent reserve.

This would suggest in turn that his equally tenacious policy of anonymity concerning his *Treatises* was rooted in a recognition that they, too, contained strange doctrine. What is puzzling, however, is that the *Treatises* were not subjected to the criticism directed against the *Letter* or the *Reasonableness*. Is this because the *Treatises* are not in fact nearly so heterodox as the other two works? But if that is the case, then why Locke's persistent anonymity? Alternatively, is there a heterodoxy in the *Treatises* but one that is more carefully concealed than that in the other two works? It is not easy to demonstrate that the latter possibility is the true one: By its very nature, a partially concealed heterodoxy appears, on the surface, mostly as orthodoxy. Thus, one has to scrutinize such a text with more than ordinary care.[6]

Given Locke's circumstances and conduct, I suggest that his great reticence concerning his *Treatises* may have reflected an awareness, first, that the book contains a strange doctrine on government hidden beneath a surface of orthodoxy; second, that it was therefore not desirable for the book to be connected to other books by him, some of them much more openly unorthodox in content, as the *Letter* surely is; third, that the *Treatises* are part of a large, overall design, a design meant to be translated into practice by the cumulative effect of his major published works but one which, too openly stated, might have brought him at least the calumny heaped on Hobbes if not the axe inflicted on Sidney.

II. The Design and Strategy of Persuasion of Locke's Main Works

I believe that Locke conceived of his major works as part of just such a coherent design. His object was to bring about a

[6]For a general discussion of such writing, see Leo Strauss, *Persecution and the Art of Writing*, (Glencoe, Ill.: 1952).

new human condition, one in which mankind would become much more at home in this world than ever before by becoming the conqueror of a penurious and largely hostile natural condition. Locke sought to achieve that object by a strategy of persuasion directed largely at the leaders of society. The strategy combined fairly open challenges to orthodoxy, as in the doctrine on toleration in the *Letter,* and more restrained, ambiguous challenges, as in the doctrines on the law of nature, on property, and on the object of government in the *Treatises.* I will now show more exactly what I mean both by the overall design and the strategy of persuasion, for it is in that framework that the *Treatises* may be most profitably understood.

The purpose of the *Letter* was to establish the "just bounds" between a "commonwealth" (or "the state," as we now say) and a "church." The commonwealth, Locke argued, is constituted solely for the "procuring, preserving, and advancing" of men's "civil interests." Civil interests, in turn, fall into two basic categories: first, the things that naturally pertain to the individual, his "life, liberty, health, and indolency [ease and rest of the] body"; second, things external to the body, such as "money, land, houses, furniture, and the like." On the other hand, the church, he argued, is a purely voluntary "society" that men may join in order publicly to worship God as "they judge acceptable to Him." Its ultimate purpose is to effect "the salvation of their souls."

The intended short-range effect of this distinction is, first, to reserve to the government the exclusive power to inflict punishment, civil or criminal, and absolutely to restrict punishment to acts committed against other men's civil interests; and second, to reserve to the church the exclusive power to discipline its members and absolutely to restrict discipline to "exhortations, admonitions, and advices," or in an extreme case, separation from the church. But the intended long-range effect is also twofold and complementary: first, wholly to secularize government and to depoliticize religion, and second, to reorient men primarily in the direction of their civil interests, which is to say in the direction of concern for their life, liberty, and possessions, the interests to be protected by government.

Locke was profoundly aware that to bring about so radical a change in the human condition would require a commensurately radical change in men's understanding of what constitutes the good life, and that this in turn would require a change in understanding principally among the leading members of society. According to Locke, they point the way for and shape the opinions of the great majority. In short, Locke's design required him to persuade the leading members of society that such a change would be beneficial to all mankind.

Locke's most theoretical book, *An Essay Concerning Human Understanding,* contributes to this aspect of his design in a fundamental way. When Locke wrote the *Essay,* in the middle and latter part of the seventeenth century, the universities still strongly emphasized the teaching of ancient and Scholastic philosophy (the latter a fusion of Christian doctrine and Aristotelian philosophy). But that traditional approach to understanding the world was increasingly under a vigorous, double assault. On one side it was besieged by the philosophical arguments of works such as Francis Bacon's *Novum Organum* (1620), which Bacon conceived of as a replacement for the *organon,* or "logic," of Aristotle. Bacon projects a new *method* and a new *end* for all the sciences. The method is to develop highly rigorous modes of reasoning concerning 1) observations made on natural bodies in their natural state and 2) observations made on experimentally induced changes in natural bodies. The end is to develop power over nature's processes by discovering their inner character and then to use that power to produce "works"—what we now know as the products of scientific technology. On the other side the traditional understanding was besieged by the actual results of the new physics, such as Isaac Newton's *Mathematical Principles of Natural Philosophy* (1687).

Locke's *Essay* unobtrusively but decisively joins forces with Bacon and Newton. Thus, in a telling image in his "Epistle to the Reader," Locke refers to himself as removing some of the "rubbish" that "lies in the way to knowledge"—that is to say, as one who helps clear away the ancient philosophies and opens the way to the new investigation of nature that was already developing in what he calls the "commonwealth of learning," whose chief citizens are men such as "the incomparable Mr. Newton." Now

Locke's own contribution to the enterprise is this: first, to determine the exact nature and limits of human understanding and, second, to direct the purged and enlightened understanding to a concern with all those things that "may be of use to us" and in particular, the things that may contribute to "a comfortable provision for this life." (Introduction, 5) In so doing Locke seeks both to divert men of great intellect from the sterile province of Scholastic philosophic disputation and from the dangerous province of religious polemics, and to redirect them to investigations that give promise of producing those works that Bacon held out as the hope of mankind. In sum, the *Essay* seeks to make all men increasingly at home in this world by teaching their intellectual leaders the theoretical principles that should guide the new commonwealth of learning, a commonwealth dedicated to securing things of "use" to men in "this life."

It is true that Locke also speaks in the *Essay* of the life beyond this one—of a "better" life, as he at one place calls it (Introduction, 5)—thus echoing traditional Christian doctrine, which teaches that man's true life is the one after death, that comes to those who truly accept Jesus as their Saviour. But since the *Essay* is primarily concerned with natural reason, and since revelation goes beyond natural reason, the *Essay* says little about what is required to enter into that better life. For that we must turn to Locke's *Reasonableness of Christianity* (1695). Now when Locke's *Reasonableness* is set beside other great works on Christian doctrine, most notably St. Augustine's *City of God* and John Calvin's *Institutes of Christian Religion,* it becomes apparent that Locke seeks to narrow the Christian teaching in a remarkable way. The Christian teaching, Locke argues, may be reduced to one and only one article of faith: "Jesus is the Messiah." Whereas St. Augustine and Calvin might conceivably have accepted Locke's formulation as a beginning for unfolding Christian doctrine, it is inconceivable that either could have accepted his reduction of the doctrine to that single, uncomplicated principle. Nor could they have accepted his argument, already articulated in the *Letter,* that the civil magistrates could not in any way require belief even in this one article. And still less could they have accepted the central sense of Locke's *Essay,* which, as

I have indicated above, seeks to direct men's intellects above all to the production of things for use in this life. But the *Reasonableness* was an integral part of Locke's own design, for it directly addressed the question of what must be conceded—at least in the circumstances he faced—to the claims of revealed religion, while at the same time circumscribing those claims as narrowly as possible.

We come then to the *Two Treatises of Government*. In the *First Treatise* Locke demolishes Sir Robert Filmer's version of the "Divine Right of Kings" to political rule. In particular he singles out for assault the arguments and the biblical citations of Filmer's *Patriarcha* (1680), in which Sir Robert sought to derive all legitimate political rule from fatherly rule and ultimately from the rule of the first father of humankind, Adam himself. In this part of the *Treatises* Locke relies mainly on refutations of Filmer's interpretation of biblical teachings and secondarily on arguments and evidence obtained from natural reason. In the *Second Treatise* Locke moves from demolition to reconstruction: He now presents his own positive teaching on the "true original, extent, and end of civil government." In this part of the *Treatises* Locke relies mainly on arguments and evidence obtained from natural reason and secondarily on what appears to be the true—as contrasted to Filmer's false —interpretations of biblical teachings. It remains to be seen whether this second element is in the final analysis compatible with the first. But it suffices for now to make two observations: First, the marked shift in emphasis from the *First Treatise* to the *Second Treatise*—the shift that brings natural reason's discoveries concerning the nature of government into the foreground—reinforces the secular sense of the commonwealth that was articulated in the *Letter Concerning Toleration*. Second, the *Second Treatise* constitutes the political cornerstone of the new edifice that Locke seeks to raise. And embedded in that cornerstone is the definitive treatment of "civil interests": It is Locke's analysis of the nature of "property," on which everything else in the work at last comes to rest.

Finally, there is the work entitled *Some Thoughts Concerning Education* (1693). Its purpose is to set forth principles for the physical, moral, and academic instruction of young men, or to be more exact, of young gentlemen. As such, the work focusses on the proper training of those individuals most likely to be among the leading part of a well-ordered political society—men of good families, of fairly extensive real property, and of good educational backgrounds, hence men having extensive "civil interests" in Locke's sense of that phrase, and therefore bound to have a considerable stake in the right ordering of government. The *Thoughts* is thus a supplement to both the *Reasonableness* and the *Second Treatise.* It is a supplement to the former in that it supplies a secular moral counterpart to the religious moral doctrine conveyed in the *Reasonableness.* It is a supplement to the latter in that it supplies guidelines for the education of those most likely to have the greatest interest in and capability of maintaining a civil government dedicated to the protection of men's life and liberty, as well as possessions such as land, houses, and money.

As we turn now to look more closely at the *Two Treatises of Government,* the reader may profitably be reminded that the work is best perceived as part of a larger design, whereby Locke seeks to give practical form to the root distinction between this-worldly and other-worldly things. Stated even more pointedly, the *Second Treatise* seeks to make men much more at home in *this* world by teaching them how to construct a civil government that will be essentially the protector of men's property, and that will, in particular, provide encouragement and protection to those "industrious" and "rational" men (*Second Treatise,* para. 34, hereafter II.34) who will most efficaciously extract a plenitude of useful goods from the penurious hand of nature.

III. An Analytical Outline of the *Two Treatises of Government.*

A. THE *FIRST TREATISE.*

The *First Treatise* is, as was noted above, a polemic against Sir Robert Filmer's patriarchal version of the "Divine Right of Kings." Locke singles out Filmer's contention that men are not "naturally free" as the key issue, for that is the "ground" or premise on which Filmer erects his argument that all legitimate government is "absolute monarchy," which descends from the first man, Adam. Early in the *First Treatise* (I.3) Locke denies that either "Scripture or reason" supports Filmer's premise and argument. In what follows, painstaking, minute biblical exegeses, treating many key Old Testament passages, such as *Genesis* 1:28, 3:16, and 9:2, dominate the polemic, suggesting that the appeal to Scripture, which contains "the revealed law of God" (I.124) has the highest priority in refuting Filmer. Conversely, the appeal to "the law of nature," or simply "nature," or again, "reason," is, throughout, in a very subordinate position. But scrutiny of the *First Treatise* reveals a reflection on nature that adumbrates that of the *Second Treatise.* In particular, in Chapter VI, which is at the center of the *First Treatise,* Locke says that there is a "general rule which nature teaches all things—of self-preservation" (I.56)—and that "all that share in the same common nature, faculties and powers, are in nature equal, and ought to partake in the same common rights and privileges." Later, extending this line of thought, he says that the "first and strongest desire" in human beings, and the one that is "wrought into the very principles" of their nature, is the desire for "self-preservation" (I.86–88).

B. THE *SECOND TREATISE.*

The *Second Treatise* is really the second part of Locke's whole "book," as he calls the *Two Treatises* in the Preface to the Reader. As such the *Second Treatise* presupposes the arguments of the *First Treatise,* arguments which, as we have seen, are primarily those rooted in biblical exegeses and secondarily those rooted in natural reason. The *Second Treatise* falls into six subdivisions.

1. Chapter I. Locke begins by reducing his whole *First Treatise* to four "premises." In the first and third of these premises, Locke in effect asserts that neither natural reason ("natural right"/ "law of nature") nor revelation ("positive donation from God"/ "positive law of God") supports Filmer's teaching on government. It is worth noting

that this ordering of natural reason and revelation reverses that which occurs early in the *First Treatise* (I.3).

Locke next admits that, having demolished Filmer's false teaching, it is incumbent upon him to supply the true teaching, lest men should fall into the dangerous belief that "all government in the world is the product only of force and violence."

Locke then opens his own teaching by seeking to distinguish "political power" from four other kinds of power: that of a father over children, of a master over servants, of a husband over wife, and of a lord over slaves. In so doing Locke seems to hearken back to and draw upon a similar line of argument found in Aristotle's *Politics,* Book I, and partially transmitted to Englishmen in a work by a great Anglican divine, Richard Hooker, in his *Laws of Ecclesiastical Polity* (1594).

Locke concludes Chapter I with a definition of political power, at the core of which is the proposition that the true end of government is to "regulate" and "preserve" men's property against both internal and external threats. In a sense, the entire remainder of the *Second Treatise* is an explication and defense of that definition. I therefore suggest that the reader scrutinize the definition and hold it in mind while working through the *Second Treatise.*

2. Chapters II–VII.86 This section contains the most fundamental parts of Locke's teaching on the *bases* of government. These are its points:

a. Chapters II–IV 1) Locke begins from the premise that man is naturally without government of any kind. His expression for that condition is the "state of nature." In that state, every man is "free," in the sense of being able to order his own actions wholly independently of the will of any other man. And in that state every man also is "equal" to every other man in the sense of being a member of the human species, in no way subordinate to nor a subject of any other man. Finally, however, every man is subject to the "law of nature" in the state of nature.

2) The law of nature is reason. It "wills" the "peace and preservation of all mankind," as much as this can be done. But because the law of nature, like every law that pertains to men "in this world," would be in vain if there were no one to execute its provisions and further

because there is no natural jurisdiction of one man over another, the power to execute the law of nature belongs to every man in the state of nature.

3) The state of nature is contrasted to the "state of war." This contrast is shown first by the fact that Locke devotes a separate chapter to each and second by the fact that in II.19 he speaks of "the plain difference" between the two states. The crux of the difference is this: When men live together without any common judge and do so "according to reason" (which is to say, according to the precepts of the law of nature), they are in the state of nature. But when they live together and one man uses or threatens to use force "without right" on the person of another, they are in the state of war, both where there is and is not a common judge. It thus happens that the state of war may suddenly erupt even within political society, for example, when a highwayman sets upon the person of a law-abiding citizen. In that situation, the law-abiding citizen temporarily regains the right to execute the law of nature and may kill the highwayman on the spot.

4) Those who willfully violate the law of nature in the state of nature by introducing a state of war, may rightfully be enslaved by the innocent party.

b. Chapter V 1) The teaching of both "natural reason" and "revelation" is that God has "given" the earth to "mankind in common." The great "difficulty" then is to understand how any single man may come to have "a property in anything."

2) A man's property consists first and most crucially of his own body and of the physical liberty to employ its faculties on his own behalf, and second of possessions secured by the use of the body and the mental faculties.

3) The most important kinds of possessions are, first, goods indispensable to the preservation of the body, such as food, drink, and clothing; second, land, including all its natural resources; and third, money.

4) In the state of nature, prior to the invention of money, every man has the natural right to seek to appropriate the first two kinds of property. The mode of appropriation is the mixing of his labor with natural materials, such as by picking wild plums or enclosing, clearing,

and tilling virgin land. The natural law limitation on such appropriation is that he must leave enough and as good in common for others to exert their labor on, and that he must not permit anything appropriated by his labor to spoil.

5) In the state of nature, after and as a result of the invention of money (which is to say, men "consent" to make money the common medium of exchange for all goods that have intrinsic worth, such as food or land), every man comes by a conventional right to heap up as much money as he chooses, for such activity does not violate the natural-law restriction on appropriation. Thus, in the state of nature the extent of property is set first by the law of nature and second by human convention, based on consent, which overcomes the restrictions set by the law of nature. But in the state of political society, the extent of property is set by the positive laws, which, however, should reflect the teaching of the state of nature, including the teaching that men have consented to an "inequality of private possessions" by the invention of money.

c. Chapters VI–VII.86 The power of parents over children is limited to caring for the young until they are of age and can care for themselves. The power of a husband over a wife is a reciprocal power rooted in the compact of a marriage. Both sorts of power are essentially different from that of political power.

3. Chapters VII.87–XIV. This section elaborates the nature of political power and that of *legitimate* government. Its main points are these:

a. Political power, or the right to make positive laws for the political society and to carry on foreign relations, comes into being, as legitimate government, *via* a "compact," or agreement, among free and equal men. Every man must give his consent to the establishment of the political society in order for it to be a legitimate "community." But every man, by this consent, also consents to the principle that the "act of the majority" shall "pass" for "the act of the whole" in the adoption of positive laws.

b. The object of legitimate government is to provide an impartial, superior force to protect men and their possessions against internal and external threats.

c. Internally the means to that end is the legislation and execution of known, settled, and specific laws—such as laws against murder or theft—with known, concrete penalties, including the death penalty.

d. Externally the means to that end is the provision for and carrying out of a viable foreign policy.

e. Political power is differentiated into three specific forms: legislative, executive, and federative (the power to carry on foreign relations). Of these three the legislative power is the "supreme" power in every legitimate government, for it is the power to make the laws that are to be executed.

f. The legislative power may be placed in the hands of many (democracy) or few (oligarchy), or one (monarchy).

g. Ordinarily the exercise of political power must be according to antecedent laws, but in cases where no laws apply easily or at all—such as the conduct of foreign policy—the government may use discretion, called "prerogative."

4. Chapter XV. This chapter recapitulates the fundamental distinction among political, despotic, and paternal power.

5. Chapters XVI–XVIII. This section elaborates the nature of *illegitimate* government. It specifies three forms of such illegitimacy:

a. unjust foreign conquest (an unprovoked attack and then a destruction of the legitimate government and its replacement by arbitrary rule).

b. internal usurpation of political rule by anyone not properly elected to office.

c. tyrannical extension of power by those who were originally properly elected.

6. Chapter XIX. This section delineates the conditions in which "the people" may legitimately "replace governments" that have been "dissolved" or have become illegitimate. The key condition is this: The people may act to replace the existing government whenever it fails to protect or, worse still, actively invades their property, which is the foundation of their "freedom" and to which each man has a natural right.

IV. On the Interpretation, the Main Emphasis, and the Truth of Locke's Political Teaching.

Locke's political teaching, like that of every great philosopher, has engendered hotly disputed questions: What exactly does Locke mean by certain key terms and lines of argument? What is the main emphasis of his teaching? Is his teaching true?

I believe that the last question is by far the most difficult of the three, and that the answer to it is the only one that ultimately matters, as I will show presently. In what follows, I will begin with the question of what exactly Locke means by the natural condition of man. I will then show that an answer to that question throws light on the question of the main emphasis of his teaching. And I will conclude with some observations on the Marxist challenge to the truth of Locke's teaching, hence to the basis for and the continuance of Western liberal democracies, insofar as they rest on a Lockean foundation.

A. ON THE PROBLEM OF WHAT LOCKE TEACHES CONCERNING MAN'S NATURAL CONDITION.

Locke clearly teaches that all men are originally in a state of nature and under the law of nature. But what exactly he means by this is not easy to say, as appears from a comparison of two interpretations.

One interpretation was offered by Basil Willey, an esteemed twentieth-century historian of ideas who summarized part of his reading of Locke by saying, "The 'State of Nature,' in Locke, is so far from resembling the 'ill condition' described by Hobbes, that it approximates rather to the Eden of the religious tradition, or the golden age of the poets . . ."[7]

[7]Basil Willey, *The Seventeenth Century Background* (New York: Columbia University Press, 1950), pp. 266–67.

The contrasting interpretation is one made by Viscount Bolingbroke, an English statesman and writer who became Secretary of War the year Locke died (1704). Bolingbroke observes that Locke himself calls the proposition that all men have a natural right to "execute the law of nature" a "strange doctrine" (II. 9, 13). He then argues that Locke had good reason so to characterize that right. For since it is, in effect, also the absolute right of every man to be judge in his own case and to punish offenders as he sees fit, what will prevent the state of nature from constantly descending in fact into a state of war? Bolingbroke answers that nothing can prevent this, hence that "[Locke's] state of freedom, [as] he calls it, would have been a state of war and violence, of mutual and alternate oppression, as really as that which Hobbes imagined to have been the state of nature."[8]

Clearly, it is impossible to reconcile these readings. But how to account for such a huge discrepancy? And what difference does it make which is the correct—or at least more nearly correct—one?

Let us begin with the second question: If Willey's reading is correct, it follows that Locke teaches that man is *naturally* in a virtual paradise: Man himself is sociable, rational, peaceful, law-abiding, and altruistic, and his condition is one of natural plenty. But if Bolingbroke's reading is correct, it follows that Locke teaches that man is *naturally* in a virtual hell: Man himself is unsociable, passionate, warlike, anarchic, and selfish, and his condition is one of natural penury. Surely it makes a profound difference which interpretation is the correct one: In Willey's reading, man's natural condition is so blessed that it is a good question why government is even needed. But in Bolingbroke's reading, man's natural condition is so wretched that the only real question is how the government that is indispensable to overcoming the natural wretchedness can most effectively be established.

[8]Viscount Bolingbroke, *Political Writings*, edited by Isaac Kramnick (New York: Meredith Corporation, 1970), pp. 12–13.

In considering which is the sounder reading of Locke, the student should reflect on these points: First, Locke's meaning is by no means everywhere easy to grasp. This is so not simply because Locke treats difficult questions but also because he sometimes writes in an involved and reticent manner. He does this, above all, when treating touchy questions such as the relationship of his own teaching to that of traditional Christian and classical teachings on natural law, property, and the end of government. Second, early in his *First Treatise* (I.7) Locke curiously likens Filmer's *way* of writing about patriarchalism to the activity of a "wary physician": Just as such a physician dilutes harsh-tasting medicine in a great quantity of something sweet-tasting, so Filmer dilutes the harshest facets of his patriarchial authority by scattering and involving his meaning, and not least, by misquoting or otherwise misusing authoritative writings, above all, the Bible. Now, Locke himself was a physician. He also was wary. And he conceived a great but in his own time essentially unorthodox design for the fundamental reordering of human life by making men at home in this world. It may then be that Locke is himself the wary physician, seeking to bring about that reordering by at least partially concealing some harsh new truths in the sugarcoating of ancient beliefs. As the reader turns eventually to scrutinize Locke's *Second Treatise* for himself, that image of the wary physician, I suggest, may profitably be his constant guide. It certainly has been my own guide in forming the judgment that Willey reads Locke's treatment of the state of nature primarily on the surface, that Bolingbroke reads it much more deeply, by probing beneath the surface, and that the latter reading is thus much closer to the truth than the former.

1. Locke's state of nature: Surface. When one scans the surface of the *Second Treatise*—and particularly, the surface of the opening, crucial chapters (Chapters I–VI)—one notices that Locke draws on observation and reason, on the authority of biblical teachings, and on other learned authority. The surface thus indicates that Locke carries on the traditional treatment of government—for example, the kind of treatment that appears in Hooker's highly traditional *Laws of Ecclesiastical Polity.*

Let us look at an example of how Locke proceeds. Near the beginning of the chapter on the state of nature he argues that "nothing is more evident" than that "creatures of the same species and rank promiscuously born to all the same advantages of nature, and the use of the same faculties, should also be equal one amongst another without subordination or subjection." This statement, which argues from evidence available to natural reason, is at once followed by a caveat cast in the form of a traditional reference to God—viz., no subjection of one man to another can take place "unless the lord and master of them all" should manifestly set one over another.

Locke next appeals to authority to prove that his contention concerning "equality of men by nature" is a valid one —the authority of "the judicious *Hooker,*" as Locke deferentially calls him (II.5). Both in Locke's comments on Hooker's teaching and in the actual quotation from Hooker great stress is placed on words and phrases resonant with the ancient teachings, philosophical as well as religious: obligation, mutual love, duties, great maxims of justice and charity, and natural duty.

Next, in Section 6, as if to reinforce by further argument what he has just derived from authority, Locke insists that men in the natural state have "liberty" but not "licence"; that they all are under the law of nature, and "the workmanship of one omnipotent, and infinitely wise maker"; and that they therefore are neither subject to one another nor entitled "to destroy one another." In short, the dominant principle seems to be the natural *duty* of men to do "justice" and to "preserve the rest of mankind."

In Sections 7–12, Locke combines arguments concerning each man's right to execute the law of nature with a further appeal to authority. That appeal takes two forms: On the one hand he resorts to traditional legal reasoning concerning the nature of law; on the other hand he draws on the Bible.

The core of the argument is this: Law, to be effective, must be enforced; and to be enforced, there must be someone to enforce it. In elaborating this argument Locke repeatedly employs words and phrases resonant with the sense of traditional legal reasoning: law, transgression, punishment, reason, common equity, reparation, restraint, offender, and execution. But beyond these, weighty as they are, there are other words that appeal to the supreme authority, the Bible itself. Thus, in Section 11 Locke says that the "rule" of "reason and common equity" is "that measure God has set to the actions of men, for their mutual security." And at the end of Section 11 he vividly draws on the story of Cain and Abel (*Genesis* 4) to give support to his doctrine.

In Sections 13–16 Locke formulates and answers two objections that might be raised against what he has been arguing. The first concerns the right to execute the law of nature, and the second concerns the actuality of men in the state of nature. In formulating and answering the objections, Locke again refers to the ultimate authority of the biblical teaching concerning the origins of government ("God hath certainly appointed government to restrain the partiality and violence of men": Section 13), and again draws on the great "authority of the judicious *Hooker*" (Section 15), who is quoted at some length.

2. Locke's state of nature: Depths.

a. Problematic Use of Authority. Locke was fully aware that the great majority of readers of his time expected that a treatise on government would appeal to the authority of works such as Hooker's *Laws* and, most crucial, the Bible. Our preceding brief look at the surface of Chapter II has shown that Locke certainly makes that appeal—or at least seems to make it. The hard question is whether the appeal is genuine or superficial—whether, that is, the appeal is rooted in a serious dependence on the teachings of Hooker and the Bible, or is a way of masking heterodoxy in orthodoxy. To answer that question requires the reader to restore the passages in Hooker and the Bible to their original context, to think through what each passage means in that context, and to return to Locke's use of the passage. In short, the hard but inescapable task is to contrast the exact sense of Locke's argument, including its *seeming* dependence on authority, with the exact sense, in context, of the authoritative passages. I will illustrate what then comes to light by a brief analysis of Locke's use of passages from *Genesis*.

At the end of Section 11 Locke sets down two brief, italicized sentences: *Who so sheddeth mans blood, by man shall his blood be shed;* and *Everyone that findeth me, shall slay me.* Neither sentence is identified as a biblical quotation, though it is at once apparent, in context, that the second sentence was spoken by Cain. Locke thus offhandedly, one might say, appeals to *Genesis,* the most crucial part of the Old Testament apart from the Ten Commandments (*Exodus* 20). Indeed, Locke does not even bother to cite the location of the sentences, relying perhaps on the reader's memory, given the famous nature of the passages. So let us look more closely.

Close examination of Chapter II reveals these pertinent facts concerning the two biblical quotations in Section 11:

1) They are the *only* direct quotations from the Bible in Chapter II and thus, one might conjecture, the most critical part of the appeal to that supreme authority.

2) They bear upon the most critical part of Locke's doctrine concerning the state of nature—the right of every man to execute the law of nature.

3) They are, or seem to be, very precisely located in the argument concerning that right: Locke first states the right in Sections 7 and 8. At the very beginning of Section 9 he admits that some may call it "a very strange doctrine." Near the end of Section 11 he gives the two biblical quotations, which seem to be appeals to supreme authority concerning the existence and character of the right. At the very beginning of Section 13, he now himself calls it a "strange doctrine." It thus happens that the biblical quotations are in what is literally the central section (9, 10, *11,* 12, 13) of a five-section sequence that is rhetorically integrated first by the theme of the right to execute the law of nature and second by the repeated, curious phrase, "strange doctrine."[9] What are we to make of all this?

Let us start again from the circumstances Locke faced: In order for any treatise on civil government to be generally acceptable to the reigning powers—political, religious, and educational—it had to be, or appear to be, consistent with the account in *Genesis* of man's beginnings. Specifically, then, the right to execute the law of nature had to be, or appear to be, consistent with that orthodox, definitive ac-

[9]Cf. Cicero, *On Oratory,* 2. 137.

count. The question then comes to this: Is Locke's doctrine on the natural right to execute the law of nature in *reality* or only in *appearance* consistent with what is taught in *Genesis?*

The signal, I suggest, that it is more appearance than reality is the twice-repeated phrase "strange doctrine," a phrase that ought to lead the reader to look anew at what is taught in the Bible. In the first place, there is no reference anywhere in *Genesis*—as can be seen by an examination of a concordance to the Bible—to "law of nature" or any "right to execute" that law. Hence, at very least Locke must be engaged in a very loose construction of *Genesis* when he boldly claims in Section 11, that the sentence "Who so sheddeth man's blood, by man shall his blood be shed" is "the great law of nature." In the second place, the biblical sentence does *not* mean in context (*Genesis* 9, especially versuses 5 and 6) that men have a right to execute the law of nature, but that God—as part of the Noahic Covenant and for the *very first* time—has given men power to execute others for murder. Furthermore, one must reflect on the profound contrast that appears between what Locke and what *Genesis* teach concerning the reason for the right to execute men: Locke teaches that it is because the law of nature otherwise will not be observed; *Genesis* teaches that it is because all men are made in "the image of God," hence that anyone who dares to murder another must himself suffer death, a reason about which Locke is simply silent. In the third place, when one turns to scrutinize Locke's second quotation a further profound contrast appears: Locke amply notices that Cain cried out, "Every one that findeth me shall slay me," and claims that that terrible cry reveals that the right to "destroy such a criminal [Cain]" was "writ in the hearts of all mankind." Perhaps so. But in *Genesis* the real significance of Cain's anguished cry appears in the very next verse, which Locke fails to quote: "And the Lord said unto him, Therefore whosoever slayeth Cain, Vengeance shall be taken on him sevenfold. And the Lord set a mark upon Cain, lest any finding him should kill him." (*Genesis* 4:15)

To sum up: Locke's appeal to the supreme authority of *Genesis* proves to be absolutely problematic, at the very least. The core of the problem is whether it is possible to square Locke's key teaching that there is a universal, perpetual right to execute men under the law of nature with the biblical teaching that *no* right whatever to execute men existed until the Noahic Covenant, long after the beginning of mankind. If not, then one must seriously consider the alternative possibility, that Locke artfully appeals to the authority of the Bible to mask a heterodoxy that he chooses not to state openly.

b. Careful Use of Phrasing. Two examples here must suffice. In the sentence that introduces the first quotation from Hooker (Section 5, beginning), Locke praises Hooker, asserts that Hooker "looks upon" the equality of men by nature as "evident in itself" and "beyond all question," and concludes with a series of three uses of the pronoun "he" in conjunction with a verb: "*he* makes," "*he* builds," and "*he* derives." (Emphasis supplied.) At the core of that series of three uses of *he* is this thought: *Hooker* makes the duties of men rest on the divinely-ordained obligation of mutual love and derives from that obligation the great maxims of justice and charity. Locke is simply silent as to whether *he himself* also understands men's duties in that way, through the impression conveyed by the whole sentence, especially when it is quickly read in context, is that that surely must be true. But when one tries to think through every step of the argument that follows and, above all, when one realizes that as the chapter progresses, "right" comes to replace "duty" as the key term of moral discourse, it begins to appear that Locke's and Hooker's understandings of the nature of moral principle may be essentially different. The reasonable conclusion is that Locke has used careful phrasing to blur that essential difference, yet leave it visible to close examination.

The second example bears on the same issue. The last sentence of Section 6 is preceded by a great rhetorical emphasis on "law of nature," "reason," "omnipotent, and infinitely wise maker," and "community of nature." And the last sentence itself lays stress on the notion that every man should seek "to preserve the rest of mankind," and "do justice." But at its core is this compelling principle, huddled among the complex set of phrases and clauses that go to make up the entire sentence: Every man should seek to preserve others "when his own preservation comes *not* into competition" (Emphasis supplied). That exception, discreetly hedged about, proves on reflection to mean that every man has an absolute right but no absolute duty, and that that absolute right is rooted in what Locke long before, discreetly hedged about in the *First Treatise* with many exegeses of Scripture and had called the "first" and "strongest" human desire, the desire to be preserved.

c. Careful Use of Structure. Locke's teaching on man's natural condition with respect to property is most fully developed in Chapter V, "Of Property." That chapter requires as close an examination as I have just given to certain aspects of Chapter II. But for present purposes I will treat just one dimension of Chapter V, Locke's very careful use of structure. I will argue that the purpose of this rhetorical device is to present an argument that very gradually undermines the Judeo-Christian teaching of God's providence with respect to the goods needful for human life.

On its surface the chapter on property is the most pious chapter in the *Second Treatise.* It begins with a marked emphasis on God's providence, as shown by both natural reason and revelation. It contains numerous references to biblical passages, to God, and to Old Testament figures, beginning with Adam. It spreads these various references widely and thus conveys the sense of a teaching on property that is rooted in biblical authority.

Close inspection shows, however, that the appeal to biblical authority is confined to ten of the first fifteen sections (25–39), and that in the last twelve sections (40–51), Locke falls utterly silent about the Bible. The seven sections that refer to God thus all fall within the first part of the chapter. In the fourth section that refers to God (31), Locke quotes a passage from the New Testament, *1 Timothy* 6:17, for the only time in Chapter V. With the help of a partial quotation from St. Paul, Locke teaches that nature's goods were given to men "to enjoy." But attentive reading of *1 Timothy* shows that St. Paul teaches in sharp contrast that men should not trust riches of this world but riches of the spirit, laid up for the life to come. Thus even within the first part of the chapter, where the biblical authority seems dominant, Locke's treatment of property is in tension with the Christian teaching. As we shall now see, that tension profoundly increases as the argument moves into the second part of the chapter.

1) Articulation of the argument concerning man's labor on nature's goods. Having at first suggested the traditional notion of God's infinite providence, Locke, beginning in Section 27, indicates the need for human labor to be exerted on the goods provided by the "spontaneous hand of nature." As the chapter progresses, the contribution of labor increases in an astonishing way, even as the biblical references recede. In Section 37, two sections after the references to God cease, Locke sets the ratio of what labor adds to nature at ten to one and then at one hundred to one. In Section 40, one section after all the biblical references cease, Locke definitely sets the ratio at one hundred to one. And in Section 43, well into the second part of the chapter, he increases the ratio to one thousand to one. This constitutes the third stage in what proves, on reflection, to be an exact geometric progression, the stages of which are articulated exactly at three-section intervals. As the authority of the Bible fades from view and then disappears altogether, human labor's addition to nature increases geometrically at a persistent ratio of ten to one.

2) Articulation of the argument concerning the nature and effect of the invention of money. At the end of the first section of Chapter V Locke says that he will seek to show "how men might come to have a *property*" in various parts of that which was given to "mankind in common," without any need for the "express compact of all the commoners." Thus, in the initial statement of the thesis of Chapter V Locke is silent about money. That aspect of the argument emerges only in the twelfth section of the chapter and then only in the form of an indication that Locke will "by and by" show how the invention of money "introduced [by consent] larger possessions, and a *right to them.*" (Emphasis supplied)

Three points are worth noting about this emergence of an argument concerning the invention of money in Section 36. First, Section 36 marks a new beginning of the argument on property, for Locke now radically alters the original thesis of Section 25. Second, Section 36 is very artfully placed: It immediately *follows* the last section in which references to God appear and immediately *precedes* the first section in which the mathematical ratios of what labor adds to nature appear. Third, Section 36 states the new thesis concerning property, but the argument in support of the thesis is delayed until Sections 45–50. The argument thus begins only after the statement of the final ratio (1000–1) in the geometric progression of what labor adds to nature, and close attention to the substance of the argument shows that it builds upon the sense of that progression.

This brief, closer look at the chapter on property indicates that Locke structured his line of reasoning so that, first, the argument for the extraordinary productive power of labor on the "almost worthless" goods of nature comes gradually to the fore as the appeal to the biblical teaching of God's providence recedes, and second, the argument for the even more extraordinary productive power of the invention of money succeeds to and draws out the full implications of the emphasis on human labor.

B. ON THE MAIN EMPHASIS OF LOCKE'S POLITICAL TEACHING.

Locke's political teaching has two main foci: man in the state of nature and man in political society. The transition from the first to the second condition is tersely summarized in the phrase "original compact" (II. 97). *Compact* signifies mutual agreement. *Original* signifies that the agreement originates or—to use the verb Locke repeatedly chooses—*makes* a political society (II. 14, 95, 96, 97, 106.). The question now is how to construe this compact, which effectuates the transition from the natural to the political condition, and the character of the latter condition once achieved. To come to grips with this question it will be helpful first to look more closely at what Locke teaches to be the end of government and second at what he means by compact and invention (for the two are closely related, as we shall see).

Locke's first definition of political power (II.3) indicates that the end of positive law is the "regulating and preserving of property." However, when he turns at the beginning of Chapter II to explicate and defend his definition, Locke at once places the theme of man's natural freedom in the foreground. Furthermore, during the chapters that prepare the way for, and are the foundation of, the chapter on property—the chapters on the state of nature, the state of war, and slavery—man's freedom retains that paramount position. Most often it is treated as natural freedom rooted in the law of nature and occasionally as political freedom rooted in the positive laws of a political society. On the other hand, Locke only once in these three chapters explicitly refers to property (II.6) and only very occasionally refers to the ordinary sense of property as "possessions" or "goods" (II.6, 11, 18, 19). In sum, throughout these chapters that establish the basis of Locke's teaching on the purpose of political society, freedom, not property, is paramount.

In the chapter on property Locke is silent about freedom, whether natural or political. When he speaks again on freedom in Chapter VI, he first reminds us of every man's original right to his "natural freedom" (II.54) and then restates the end of law: "Law, in its true notion, is not so much the limitation as the direction of a free and intelligent agent to his proper interest"; and "the end of law is not to abolish or restrain, but to preserve and enlarge freedom" (II.57).

This restatement of the end of law as freedom surely stands in some tension with the original statement of the end of law as the regulation and preservation of property. It seems, as one reflects on this tension and on the stages of the unfolding of Locke's argument, that the *immediate* end of positive laws in a properly constituted political society is the protection of men's individual property—person, liberty of action, possessions—but that the *true and ultimate* end is the protection of men's freedom, that first and natural condition of every man. Stated somewhat differently, the positive laws' protection of individual property is the necessary means to the protection of individual freedom. Furthermore, property, by being concrete, personal, and of great interest to the vast majority of men, secures their political weight on behalf of the more fundamental but essentially less tangible good, freedom.[10]

Let us return now to the notion of the original compact. Locke teaches that the compact "makes" a "body politic." His language thus suggests that the body politic is an artifact, a thing produced by human art and contrivance, though from natural materials, human beings. But human beings apparently lack any truly natural inclination to come together as a community or to be naturally political. Consequently the great problem is how to bring men from the natural into the political condition, the latter being the only condition that can truly secure the freedom that they seek. The device of the original compact—and it is important to remember that compact means mutual agreement among the multitude of men, and that such agreement is necessarily rooted in the opinions of those who enter into it—must appeal to that which the vast majority of men naturally seek and are most capable of appreciating: a comfortable, safe, and peaceable condition (II.95).

A further question now arises: Is the concept of the original compact itself natural to man? Or is it something made by man or at least by some men, even as the body politic is said to be made by the compact? Locke does not directly treat this important question in the *Second Treatise*, for it is a work of political philosophy, conveying not a theoretical analysis of the character of political concepts, but a political teaching to mankind for the achievement of human good. But Locke does give a clue to an answer in his discussion of compact and invention in the chapter on property.

In Section 45, Locke conjoins three aspects of man's activity: 1) the exertion of labor on natural goods; 2) the use of money; 3) the settling of the bounds of individual prop-

[10]The question whether "economics" or "politics" is ultimately most fundamental in Locke's teaching is one of the hotly disputed questions of contemporary scholarship. See in particular C. B. Macpherson, *The Political Theory of Possessive Individualism* (Oxford: At the Clarendon Press, 1962), Chapter V.; and Harvey C. Mansfield, Jr., "On the Political Character of Property in Locke," in A. Kontos, ed., *Powers, Possessions and Freedom: Essays in Honor of C. B. Macpherson* (Toronto: University of Toronto Press, 1979), pp. 23–38. The statement in the text is indebted to Mansfield's very thoughtful argument.

erty by compact. This conjunction and sequence are suggestive. First, the use of money, which Locke elsewhere calls an "invention," and indeed it is the only invention so-called in the chapter, proves, on reflection, to be a convention rooted in mental not physical labor. It is a convention that radically increases the productivity of physical labor, especially in conjunction with other mental labor, such as the invention of banking systems that facilitate national and international commerce, and the unleashing of human technical inventiveness. It is worth noting in this connection that in the *Essay Concerning Human Understanding* Locke says ". . . he who first made known the use of that contemptible mineral [iron], may be truly styled the father of arts, and the author of plenty." A bit later Locke praises the invention of printing and of the compass, and the discovery of the use of quinine, as having done more for mankind by far than did all those who merely built colleges, workhouses, and hospitals.[11]

Second, the original compact, as a key element in Locke's political teaching, proves on further reflection to be even more decisively a product of mental labor than does the invention of money. For the invention of money is a long, slow, and groping activity, arising out of primitive barter and the primitive use of shells or other natural objects, on which conventional value is at length bestowed. But the compact, in the form it is conveyed in Locke's political teaching, is itself the fruit of Locke's reason at work, painfully and with much application investigating the character of political things. The original compact is itself thus a human product, arising from the mental labor of Locke's thought. In the form it is taught in the *Second Treatise,* it is akin to refined gold reduced to refined iron, the latter being worked into the ligament of political society. It completes the work undertaken by the human convention of money—the work of making it possible for men to heap up unequal possessions through the free use of unequal faculties—by securing those possessions and the freedom of those faculties behind the stout fence of the positive laws, and all this for the public good.

[11]*An Essay Concerning Human Understanding*, IV. xii. 11 and 12.

The main emphasis, then, of Locke's political teaching is on the artful human construction of political institutions which will reflect the primacy and potency of the human passions to be safe, comfortable, and peaceful (II.95). The *origin* of government is the joining of wills by the convention of the original compact to form a political society. The *extent* of government is the protection of men's civil interests. The *end* of government is the removal of man from the merely natural condition to the predominantly conventional condition of a properly constituted political society. Within this latter condition, the great natural good, freedom, is finally to be secured. And human activity—physical, and above all, mental labor—is the catalyst of that astounding transformation. Reduced to its core, Locke's political teaching is that the wretchedness, stupidity, and insecurity of man's natural condition may be decisively overcome by the proper application of two most remarkable human inventions: money and the original compact.

C. ON THE PROBLEM OF THE TRUTH OF LOCKE'S TEACHING.

When Locke published his *Treatises* and his other great works, he was convinced that their teaching concerning the route to human freedom would permanently supplant that of earlier teachings, precisely because of the greater truthfulness of his own teaching. And so it seemed for quite some time, for Locke's teaching became widely accepted in the West. But what Locke seems not to have anticipated is the more and more radical teaching on nature, man, and society that would at length emerge in the writings of Rousseau, Kant, Hegel, Marx, Nietzsche, and others. Today, Locke's teaching is very much on the defensive. In the area of the social sciences in particular one form of the critique of Locke's teaching is a rather apolitical philosophical development called "positivism." Taking its bearings by what it holds to be proper scientific method, positivism makes a fundamental distinction between "facts" and "values," and it subsumes the main elements of Locke's political teaching—above all those elements that rest on the argument that man has a natural right to freedom—under prescientific "value theory" or "normative theory," thus seeking to deprive his teaching of any claim to being scientific truth, as Locke thought it to be. But given the gravity of the contemporary conflict between Lockean based liberal democracies and Marxist based communist states, I will formulate the problem concerning the truth of Locke's teaching in terms of the Marxist critique.

The Marxist critique of Locke's teaching begins with Hegel. Philosophers prior to Hegel believed that philosophy essentially transcends the particular historical and political setting in which the philosopher lives and that thus the philosopher can in principle arrive at that which is true for all times and places. But Hegel claimed to discover that all thought, including philosophy, is essentially "historical" in nature: The philosopher's supreme efforts are but the refined, ordered distillation and expression of the "spirit of the times" in which the philosopher chances to live. Thus Plato believed that he had arrived at the truth, good for all times and places, when he argued in *The Republic* that the best rule is that of philosopher-kings. But Hegel argues that Plato's teaching is but an expression of the essence of the "spiritual" forms coming to be within the historical process during the epoch of the Greek *polis:* Just as the *polis* is a historical political form now forever superceded, so is Plato's philosophy a historical moment in the unfolding history of philosophy that is also now forever superceded.

It remained for Marx, however, to push Hegel's "historicization" of all thought to its proper conclusion. For Marx, turning Hegel's doctrine on its head, as he said, argues that all prior philosophy is not an expression of historically emergent spirit but an "ideology," which is to say an unconscious rationalization of the rule of the dominant class of that epoch, of the political forms through which such rule takes place, and above all of the material forces of production on which the dominance rests. Thus Aristotle believed that he had arrived at the political truth when he argued that it is both just and prudent to settle rule on the citizens of some wealth and stake in the *polis,* and that such men rightly may make use of "natural" slaves to tend to their household economy. But Marx argues that this teaching is but an unconscious rationalization of the slave economy on which the ancient *poleis* rested.[12]

Applied specifically to Locke's teaching, the Marxist critique[13] recognizes Locke as a modern "materialist"—that is, as one who holds that reality is to be understood essentially in terms of the activities and processes of material nature. Modern materialism in turn is the ideological superstructure of emergent technologically oriented science, and of capitalism, which utilizes that science for its own rapacious ends—for example, to build weapons with which to subdue backward peoples and plunder their resources. As for Locke's political teaching in particular, it is the essence of the ideological superstructure of the modern capitalist state. First, Locke's claim that man's natural condition is one of insecurity and penury is not true of man as such; it is merely an ideological expression of man's severe "alienation" from his true self under emergent capitalism, that is, of his estrangement from his true relationship to nature, as the rightful joint owner, conqueror, and user of its resources, and worse still of his terrible estrangement from his fellow men. Second, Locke's claim that all men have an original natural right to private property, and that that right must be made practically effective by the laws of properly constructed political societies is an ideological expression of the essential selfishness of the emergent dominant class, the bourgeoisie. Third, Locke's claim that elected, representative government is the best guarantor that the people will control those who make and execute the laws is an ideological expression both of the self-deception of the bourgeoisie and of its ability to dupe the great majority of the citizenry into believing that such is the case. Fourth, Locke's claim that the laws' protection of individual property constitutes the fence to individual freedom is but the ideological expression of false freedom.

The Marxist critique of Locke's political teaching constitutes a formidable challenge to the long-range political via-

[12]*See* Karl Marx, *Capital: A Critique of Political Economy* (New York: Random House, n.d.), pp. 68–69.

[13]Marx himself wrote very little about Locke's teaching. The argument in the text refers to later writers who are followers of Marx.

bility of liberal democracies. For by its claim to have shown the merely "ideological" character of natural rights, representative government, the right to private property, and the right to individual freedom, it seeks to tear away the foundations of the political institutions of those regimes, and as those foundations crumble, so, at last, must the regimes. That prospect is reason enough today for students to give the most careful attention to Locke's own argument in support of his teaching; for in so doing, they may come to an independent judgment concerning the truth of his own claims, a judgment indispensable to thinking about and weighing the criticisms directed against it.

But the problem is not simply a political one. For the Marxist critique of Locke's understanding of philosophy is, as we have seen, but a special case of its sweeping critique of all philosophical systems, indeed, of all philosophizing prior to that of Marx. It is perhaps not too much then to say that that critique constitutes a challenge to the future existence of philosophizing as such. Philosophy as a word and as an activity of the human soul emerged in ancient Greece. Its original meaning is "love of wisdom." And "wisdom" means complete or final understanding of the nature of all things—for example, of heavenly bodies, the earth, animals, man, motion, number, and being. Wisdom, so understood, is conceived of as being the end or proper ultimate object of the human soul, but an end that is problematically realizable. It follows that the activity of philosophizing is intrinsically more capable of being realized than is the end that it seeks. It also follows that the truly good political regime is one that explicitly and deliberately ensures that philosophizing is made possible for those capable of engaging in it.

Modernity begins with a critique of the ancient understanding of the nature of human reason and of the significance of the contemplative life for setting the natural standard of political life. The first phase of the critique begins with Machiavelli's "realism," as it is likely to be called today. That realism consists in calling into question the ability of reason to arrive at a comprehensive understanding of the principles of things, and in replacing the contemplative life as the end of the good regime with ends that political men everywhere and at all times seek: honor, rule, prosperity, empire, and ultimately, glory. Locke follows the route to "new modes and orders" that had been opened by Machiavelli. For Locke argues that reason is incapable of discerning any truly natural end of man (". . .the philosophers of old did in vain inquire, whether *summum bonum* [the most perfect good] consisted in riches, bodily delights, or virtue, or contemplation. . ."[14]) but is capable of discerning the natural beginning of man, a beginning that shows man to be free by nature, free to make his way by the artful use of conventions from the state of nature into the security and comforts of political society.

The critique of the ancient understanding enters a second, more radical phase with the emergence of the Hegelian-Marxist thesis. For now, reason's ability to discern any standard in nature, even the negative one of the state of nature, comes under critical assault. Indeed, reason itself becomes an epiphenomenon of the "historical process," a mere moment in the dialectic of material forces, a mirror of the dominant and repressive ruling order of each epoch.

The problem of the truth of Locke's political teaching thus proves, on close inspection, to be the problem of the truth of his understanding of human reason—of reason's ability to discern a standard in nature, of reason's naturalness to man, of reason's access to principles that are not simply the product of human activity. With this observation, we return to the larger problem from which we began: the quarrel between the ancients and the moderns. Locke joins the ancients in understanding reason as capable of finding a standard in nature. But he even more decisively joins the moderns in understanding reason as incapable of discovering any natural end of human activity. The precarious status of reason in Locke's teaching is, then, the point at which our own use of reason is most in need of being exerted, particularly today when the undermining of reason's claims is a widespread phenomenon. We honor Locke by such an exertion even if it should happen that we must at last come reasonably to disagree with him concerning the nature of reason.

[14]*An Essay Concerning Human Understanding*, II. xxi. 56. Cf. Aristotle, *Nichomachean Ethics*, 1095b15–1096a5, and 1177a13–1179a32.

note on the text

The library of Christ's College, Cambridge University, contains a hand-corrected copy of the third (1698) printing of Locke's *Two Treatises*. Peter Laslett, in his critical edition of Locke's work (Cambridge University Press: 1967), persuasively argues that this copy is one of two "master" copies Locke left behind as the basis for a correct text. I wish to thank the Librarian of Christ's College for having supplied a photocopy of the College's text. With the assistance of Michael Mombrea, I have adapted the Christ's College text for this printing. I have modernized the spelling, but largely retained Locke's own punctuation and his extensive use of italics. I have checked my reading of the hand corrections against that of Peter Laslett.

principal dates in the life of John Locke

1632	Born at Wrington, Somerset, son of an attorney.
1647–1652	Educated at Westminster School (London).
1652–1665	Principally at Christ Church College (Oxford University), at first as undergraduate then as holder of various positions.
1665–1666	Secretary of a diplomatic mission to Brandenburg.
1666	Begins long association with Anthony Ashley Cooper, First Earl of Shaftesbury. Appointed to Studentship of Medicine at Christ Church.
1668	Elected a Fellow of the Royal Society.
1675–1678	Travels and studies in France.
1682	Shaftesbury flees to France; Algernon Sidney beheaded for treason.
1683–1689	Flees to Holland. Political refugee spending part of the time in hiding, often using disguises. Returns to England when William and Mary become King and Queen of England.

1689	Publishes *Letter on Toleration,* and *Two Treatises of Government.*
1690	Publishes *An Essay Concerning Human Understanding,* and a *Second Letter Concerning Toleration.*
1692	Publishes a *Third Letter Concerning Toleration,* and *Some Considerations of the Consequence of the Lowering of Interest, and Raising the Value of Money.*
1693	Publishes *Some Thoughts Concerning Education.*
1695	Publishes *The Reasonableness of Christianity.*
1696–1700	Serves as Commissioner of Board of Trade.
1700–1704	Lives largely in retirement at Oates, the country estate of Sir Francis and Lady Damaris Masham.
1704	Dies and is buried in the churchyard of High Laver.

Second Treatise of Government

I

1. It having been shown in the foregoing discourse,

1. That *Adam* had not, either by natural right of fatherhood, nor by positive donation from God, any such authority over his children, or dominion over the world, as is pretended.

2. That if he had, his heirs yet had no right to it.

3. That if his heirs had, there being no law of nature nor positive law of God that determines which is the right heir in all cases that may arise, the right of succession, and consequently of bearing rule, could not have been certainly determined.

4. That if even that had been determined, yet the knowledge of which is the eldest line of *Adam's* posterity being so long since utterly lost, that in the races of mankind and families of the world, there remains not to one above another, the least pretence to be the eldest house, and to have the right of inheritance.

All these premises having, as I think, been clearly made out, it is impossible that the rulers now on earth should make any benefit, or derive any the least shadow of authority from that, which is held to be the fountain of all power, *Adam's private dominion and paternal jurisdiction,* so that he that will not give just occasion to think that all government in the world is the product only of force and violence, and that men live together by no other rules but that of beasts, where the strongest carries it, and so lay a foundation for perpetual disorder and mischief, tumult, sedition, and rebellion (things that the followers of that hypothesis so loudly cry out against), must of necessity find out another rise of government, another original of political power, and another way of designing and knowing the persons that have it, than what Sir *Robert Filmer* hath taught us.

2. To this purpose, I think it may not be amiss, to set down what I take to be political power. That the power of a *magistrate* over a subject may be distinguished from that

of a *father* over his children, a *master* over his servant, a *husband* over his wife, and a *lord* over his slave. All which distinct powers happening sometimes together in the same man, if he be considered under these different relations, it may help us to distinguish these powers one from another, and show the difference betwixt a ruler of a commonwealth, a father of a family, and a captain of a galley.

3. *Political power* then I take to be *a right* of making laws with penalties of death[1] and consequently all less penalties, for the regulating and preserving of property, and of employing the force of the community, in the execution of such laws, and in the defence of the commonwealth from foreign injury; and all this only for the public good.

[1]**penalties of death:** Thus, from the outset Locke makes it clear that the imposition of the death penalty is a legitimate function of properly constituted government. The justification for such a penalty is to be found in Chapter II. It derives from every man's natural right to execute the law of nature.

II
Of the State of Nature

4. To understand political power right, and derive it from its original, we must consider what state all men are naturally in, and that is, a *state of perfect freedom* to order their actions, and dispose of their possessions and persons, as they think fit, within the bounds of the law of nature, without asking leave, or depending upon the will of any other man.

A *state* also *equality,* wherein all the power and jurisdiction is reciprocal, no one having more than another: there being nothing more evident, than that creatures of the same species and rank, promiscuously born[1] to all the same advantages of nature, and the use of the same faculties, should also be equal one amongst another without subordination or subjection, unless the lord and master of them all should, by any manifest declaration of his will, set one above another, and confer on him, by an evident and clear appointment, an undoubted right to dominion and sovereignty.

5. This *equality* of men by nature, the judicious *Hooker*[2] looks upon as so evident in itself, and beyond all question, that he makes it the foundation of that obligation to mutual love amongst men, on which he builds the duties

[1]**born:** Cf. the account of Creation in *Genesis* 1–2.

[2]***Hooker:*** This is the first of fifteen quotations from Richard Hooker, *Laws of Ecclesiastical Polity* (Book I. Section 10). The other quotations are in Sections 15, 60, 61, 74, 90, 91, 94 (2), 111, 134 (2), 135, 136 (2). All but one quotation are from Book I, entitled "Concerning Laws and Their Several Kinds in General"; ten are from Book I. Section 10, which treats civil government. Locke quotes selectively and not always exactly. The reader is urged to read Section 10, and to compare what Locke says with what Hooker says in each case.

they owe one another, and from whence he derives the great maxims *of justice* and *charity*. His words are:

'The like natural inducement hath brought men to know that it is no less their duty, to love others than themselves; for seeing those things which are equal, must needs all have one measure; if I cannot but wish to receive good, even as much at every man's hands, as any man can wish unto his own soul, how should I look to have any part of my desire herein satisfied, unless myself be careful to satisfy the like desire, which is undoubtedly in other men, being of one and the same nature? to have any thing offered them repugnant to this desire, must needs in all respects grieve them as much as me, so that if I do harm, I must look to suffer, there being no reason that others should shew greater measure of love to me, than they have by me shewed unto them; my desire therefore to be loved of my equals in nature, as much as possible may be, imposeth upon me a natural duty of bearing to themward fully the like affection; from which relation of equality between ourselves and them that are as ourselves, what several rules and canons natural reason hath drawn for direction of life, no man is ignorant.' Eccl. Pol., lib. i.

6. But though this be a *state of liberty,* yet it is *not a state of licence,* though man in that state have an uncontrollable liberty to dispose of his person or possessions, yet he has not liberty to destroy himself, or so much as any creature in his possession, but where some nobler use than its bare preservation calls for it. The *state of nature* has a law of nature to govern it, which obliges every one: And reason, which is that law, teaches all mankind, who will but consult it, that being all equal and independent, no one ought to harm another in his life, health, liberty, or possessions. For men being all the workmanship of one omnipotent, and infinitely wise maker; all the servants of one sovereign master, sent into the world by his order, and about his business, they are his property, whose workmanship they are, made to last during his, not one another's pleasure. And being furnished with like faculties, sharing all in one community of nature, there cannot be supposed any such *subordination* among us, that may authorize us to destroy one another, as if we were made for one another's uses, as the inferior ranks of creatures are for ours. Every one, as he is *bound to preserve himself,* and not to quit his station wilfully; so by the like reason, when his own preservation

comes not in competition, ought he, as much as he can, *to preserve the rest of mankind,* and may not unless it be to do justice on an offender, take away, or impair the life, or what tends to the preservation of the life, the liberty, health, limb or goods of another.

7. And that all men may be restrained from invading others rights, and from doing hurt to one another, and the law of nature be observed, which willeth the peace and *preservation of all mankind,* the *execution* of the law of nature is in that state, put into every man's hands, whereby every one has a right to punish the transgressors of that law to such a degree, as may hinder its violation. For the *law of nature* would, as all other laws that concern men in this world, be in vain, if there were nobody that in the state of nature had a *power to execute* that law, and thereby preserve the innocent and restrain offenders, and if any one in the state of nature may punish another for any evil he has done, every one may do so. For in that *state of perfect equality* where naturally there is no superiority or jurisdiction of one over another, what any may do in prosecution of that law, every one must needs have a right to do.

8. And thus, in the state of nature, *one man comes by a power over another;* but yet no absolute or arbitrary power, to use a criminal, when he has got him in his hands, according to the passionate heats, or boundless extravagancy of his own will; but only to retribute to him, so far as calm reason and conscience dictates, what is proportionate to his transgression, which is so much as may serve for *reparation* and *restraint.* For these two are the only reasons why one man may lawfully do harm to another, which is that we call *punishment.* In transgressing the law of nature, the offender declares himself to live by another rule, than that of *reason* and common equity, which is that measure God has set to the actions of men for their mutual security: and so he becomes dangerous to mankind, the tie, which is to secure them from injury and violence, being slighted and broken by him. Which being a trespass against the whole species, and the peace and safety of it, provided for by the law of nature, every man upon this score, by the right he hath to preserve mankind in general, may restrain, or where it is necessary, destroy things noxious to them, and so may bring such evil on any one, who hath transgressed

that law, as may make him repent the doing of it, and thereby deter him, and, by his example others, from doing the like mischief. And in this case, and upon this ground, every *man hath a right to punish the offender, and be executioner of the law of nature.*

9. I doubt not but this will seem a very strange doctrine to some men: but before they condemn it, I desire them to resolve me, by what right any prince or state can put to death, or *punish an alien,* for any crime he commits in their country. 'Tis certain their laws, by virtue of any sanction they receive from the promulgated will of the legislative, reach not a stranger: they speak not to him, nor if they did, is he bound to hearken to them. The legislative authority, by which they are in force over the subjects of that commonwealth, hath no power over him. Those who have the supreme power of making laws in *England, France* or *Holland,* are to an *Indian,* but like the rest of the world, men without authority: and therefore if by the law of nature every man hath not a power to punish offences against it, as he soberly judges the case to require, I see not how the magistrate of any community, can *punish an alien* of another country, since in reference to him, they can have no more power than what every man naturally may have over another.

10. Besides the crime which consists in violating the law, and varying from the right rule of reason, whereby a man so far becomes degenerate, and declares himself to quit the principles of human nature and to be a noxious creature, there is commonly *injury* done to some person or other, and some other man receives damage by his transgression, in which case he who hath received any damage, has besides the right of punishment common to him with other men, a particular right to seek *reparation* from him that has done it. And any other person who finds it just, may also join with him that is injured, and assist him in recovering from the offender, so much as may make satisfaction for the harm he has suffered.

11. From these *two distinct rights,* the one of *punishing* the crime *for restraint,* and preventing the like offence, which right of punishing is in everybody; the other of taking *reparation,* which belongs only to the injured party, comes it to pass that the magistrate, who by being magistrate hath the

common right of punishing put into his hands, can often, where the public good demands not the execution of the law, *remit* the punishment of criminal offences by his own authority, but yet cannot *remit* the satisfaction due to any private man, for the damage he has received. That, he who has suffered the damage has a right to demand in his own name, and he alone can *remit:* The damnified person has this power of appropriating to himself the goods or service of the offender, by *right of self-preservation,* as every man has a power to punish the crime, to prevent its being committed again, *by the right he has of preserving all mankind,* and doing all reasonable things he can in order to that end: And thus it is, that every man, in the state of nature, has a power to kill a murderer, both to deter others from doing the like injury, which no reparation can compensate, by the example of the punishment that attends it from every body, and also *to secure* men from the attempts of a criminal, who having renounced reason, the common rule and measure God hath given to mankind, hath by the unjust violence and slaughter he hath committed upon one, declared war against all mankind, and therefore may be destroyed as a *lion* or a *tiger,* one of those wild savage beasts, with whom men can have no society nor security: and upon this is grounded that great law of nature, *Whoso sheddeth man's blood, by man shall his blood be shed.* And Cain was so fully convinced, that every one had a right to destroy such a criminal, that after the murder of his brother, he cries out, *Every one that findeth me shall slay me;* so plain was it writ in the hearts of all mankind.[3]

12. By the same reason may a man in the state of nature *punish the lesser breaches* of that law. It will perhaps be demanded with death? I answer, each transgression may be *punished* to that *degree,* and with so much *severity* as will suffice to make it an ill bargain to the offender, give him cause to repent, and terrify others from doing the like. Every offence, that can be committed in the state of nature, may in the state of nature be also punished equally, and as far forth as it may, in a commonwealth; for though

[3]***Whoso. . .Every:*** the first two biblical quotations in the *Second Treatise;* they are from *Genesis* 9:6 and *Genesis* 4:14.

it would be besides my present purpose, to enter here into the particulars of the law of nature, or its *measures of punishment;* yet, it is certain there is such a law, and that too, as intelligible and plain to a rational creature, and a studier of that law, as the positive laws of commonwealths, nay possibly plainer; as much as reason is easier to be understood, than the fancies and intricate contrivances of men, following contrary and hidden interests put into words; for so truly are a great part of the *municipal laws* of countries, which are only so far right, as they are founded on the law of nature, by which they are to be regulated and interpreted.

13. To this strange doctrine, *viz.* That *in the state of nature every one has the executive power* of the law of nature, I doubt not but it will be objected, That it is unreasonable for men to be judges in their own cases, that self-love will make men partial to themselves and their friends. And on the other side, that ill-nature, passion and revenge will carry them too far in punishing others. And hence nothing but confusion and disorder will follow, and that therefore God[4] hath certainly appointed government to restrain the partiality and violence of men. I easily grant, that *civil government* is the proper remedy for the inconveniences of the state of nature, which must certainly be great where men may be judges in their own case, since 'tis easy to be imagined, that he who was so unjust as to do his brother an injury, will scarce be so just as to condemn himself for it: but I shall desire those who make this objection, to remember, that *absolute monarchs* are but men, and if government is to be the remedy of those evils, which necessarily follow from men's being judges in their own cases, and the state of nature is therefore not to be endured, I desire to know what kind of government that is, and how much better it is than the state of nature, where one man commanding a multitude, has the liberty to be judge in his own case, and may do to all his subjects whatever he pleases, without the least liberty to any one to question or control those who execute his pleasure? And in whatsoever he doth, whether led by reason, mistake or

[4]**God:** Cf. St. Paul's *Letter to the Romans* 13.

passion, must be submitted to? Much better it is in the state of nature wherein men are not bound to submit to the unjust will of another: And if he that judges, judges amiss in his own, or any other case, he is answerable for it to the rest of mankind.

14. 'Tis often asked as a mighty objection, *Where are,* or ever were there any *men in such a state of nature?* To which it may suffice as an answer at present; That since all *princes* and rulers of *independent* governments all through the world, are in a state of nature, 'tis plain the world never was, nor ever will be, without numbers of men in that state. I have named all governors of *independent* communities, whether they are, or are not, in league with others: For 'tis not every compact that puts an end to the state of nature between men, but only this one of agreeing together mutually to enter into one community, and make one body politic; other promises, and compacts, men may make one with another, and yet still be in the state of nature. The promises and bargains for truck, etc. between the two men in the desert island, mentioned by *Garcilasso de la Vega,*[5] in his history of *Peru,* or between a *Swiss* and an *Indian,* in the woods of *America,* are binding to them, though they are perfectly in a state of nature, in reference to one another. For truth and keeping of faith belongs to men as men, and not as members of society.

15. To those that say, There were never any men in the state of nature; I will not only oppose the authority of the judicious *Hooker, Eccl. Pol. lib. i. sect. 10,* where he says, '*the laws which have been hitherto mentioned, i.e.,* the laws of nature, *do bind men absolutely, even as they are men, although they have never any settled fellowship, never any solemn agreement amongst themselves what to do, or not to do, but forasmuch as we are not by ourselves sufficient to furnish ourselves with competent store of things, needful for such a life as our nature doth desire, a life fit for the dignity of man; therefore to supply those defects and imperfections which are in us, as living singly and solely by ourselves, we are naturally induced to seek communion and fellowship*

[5]**Vega:** Garcilasso de la Vega (c. 1540–1616) was the son of a Spanish conqueror and an Incan princess. Locke refers to his *First Part of the Royal Commentaries of the Incas*, Book I, Chapters 7–8.

with others, this was the cause of mens' uniting themselves at first in politic societies.' But I moreover affirm, That all men are naturally in that state, and remain so, till by their own consents they make themselves members of some politic society; and I doubt not in the sequel of this discourse, to make it very clear.

III
Of the State of War

16. The *state of war*[1] is a state of enmity and destruction; and therefore declaring by word or action, not a passionate and hasty, but sedate, settled design upon another man's life, *puts him in a state of war* with him against whom he has declared such an intention, and so has exposed his life to the other's power to be taken away by him, or any one that joins with him in his defence, and espouses his quarrel: it being reasonable and just I should have a right to destroy that which threatens me with destruction. For *by the fundamental law of nature, man being to be preserved,* as much as possible, when all cannot be preserved, the safety of the innocent is to be preferred: and one may destroy a man who makes war upon him, or has discovered an enmity to his being, for the same reason that he may kill a *wolf* or a *lion;* because such men are not under the ties of the common law of reason, have no other rule, but that of force and violence, and so may be treated as beasts of prey, those dangerous and noxious creatures that will be sure to destroy him whenever he falls into their power.

17. And hence it is, that he who attempts to get another man into his absolute power, does thereby *put himself into a state of war* with him; it being to be understood as a declaration of a design upon his life. For I have reason to conclude, that he who would get me into his power without my consent would use me as he pleased when he had got me there, and destroy me too when he had a fancy to it: for nobody can desire to *have me in his absolute power* unless it be to compel me by force to that, which is against the right of my freedom—*i.e.* make me a slave. To be free from such

[1]***state of war:*** Cf. Thomas Hobbes' *Leviathan*, Chapter 13.

force is the only security of my preservation: and reason bids me look on him, as an enemy to my preservation, who would take away that *freedom,* which is the fence to it: so that he who makes an *attempt to enslave me,* thereby puts himself into a state of war with me. He that in the state of nature, *would take away the freedom* that belongs to any one in that state, must necessarily be supposed to have a design to take away everything else, that *freedom* being the foundation of all the rest: as he that in the state of society, would take away the *freedom* belonging to those of that society or commonwealth, must be supposed to design to take away from them everything else, and so be looked on as *in a state of war.*

18. This makes it lawful for a man to *kill a thief,* who has not in the least hurt him, nor declared any design upon his life, any farther than by the use of force, so to get him in his power, as to take away his money, or what he pleases, from him: because using force, where he has no right to get me into his power, let his pretence be what it will, I have no reason to suppose that he who would *take away my liberty,* would not, when he had me in his power, take away everything else. And therefore it is lawful for me to treat him as one who has put *himself into a state of war* with me, *i.e.,* kill him if I can; for to that hazard does he justly expose himself whoever introduces a state of war, and is aggressor in it.

19. And here we have the plain *difference between the state of nature, and the state of war,* which however some men have confounded, are as far distant, as a state of peace, good-will, mutual assistance, and preservation, and a state of enmity, malice, violence and mutual destruction are one from another. Men living together according to reason without a common superior on earth, with authority to judge between them, is properly *the state of nature.* But force, or a declared design of force upon the person of another, where there is no common superior on earth to appeal to for relief, *is the state of war:* and 'tis the want of such an appeal gives a man the right of war even against an *aggressor,* though he be in society and a fellow-subject. Thus, a *thief,* whom I cannot harm, but by appeal to the law, for having stolen all that I am worth, I may kill when he sets on me to rob me, but of my horse or coat; because the law,

which was made for my preservation, where it cannot interpose to secure my life from present force, which if lost, is capable of no reparation, permits me my own defence, and the right of war, a liberty to kill the aggressor, because the aggressor allows not time to appeal to our common judge, nor the decision of the law, for remedy in a case where the mischief may be irreparable. *Want of a common judge with authority, puts all men in a state of nature: force without right upon a man's person makes a state of war,* both where there is, and is not, a common judge.

20. But when the actual force is over, the *state of war ceases* between those that are in society, and are equally on both sides subjected to the fair determination of the law; because then there lies open the remedy of appeal for the past injury, and to prevent future harm: but where no such appeal is, as in the state of nature, for want of positive laws, and judges with authority to appeal to, *the state of war, once begun, continues,* with a right to the innocent party to destroy the other whenever he can, until the aggressor offers peace, and desires reconcilation on such terms, as may repair any wrongs he has already done, and secure the innocent for the future: nay, where an appeal to the law, and constituted judges lies open, but the remedy is denied by a manifest perverting of justice, and a barefaced wresting of the laws, to protect or indemnify the violence or injuries of some men, or party of men, *there* it *is* hard to imagine any thing but a *state of war.* For wherever violence is used, and injury done, though by hands appointed to administer justice, it is still violence and injury, however coloured with the name, pretences, or forms of law, the end whereof being to protect and redress the innocent, by an unbiassed application of it, to all who are under it; wherever that is not *bona fide* done, *war is made* upon the sufferers, who having no appeal on earth to right them, they are left to the only remedy in such cases, an appeal to Heaven.

21. To avoid this state of war (wherein there is no appeal but to Heaven, and wherein every the least difference is apt to end, where there is no authority to decide between the contenders) is one great *reason of men's putting themselves into society,* and quitting the state of nature. For where there is an authority, a power on earth, from which relief

can be had by *appeal,* there the continuance of the state of war is excluded, and the controversy is decided by that power. Had there been any such court, any superior jurisdiction on earth, to determine the right between *Jephtha* and the *Ammonites,* they had never come to a state of war, but we see he was forced to appeal to *Heaven. The Lord the judge* (says he) *be judge this day between the Children of Israel, and the Children of Ammon. Judges* xi. 27, and then prosecuting, and relying on his *appeal,* he leads out his army to battle: And therefore in such controversies, where the question is put, *who shall be judge?* it cannot be meant, who shall decide the controversy; every one knows what *Jephtha* here tells us, that *the Lord the judge* shall judge. Where there is no judge on earth, the *appeal* lies to God in heaven. That question then cannot mean, Who shall judge? whether another hath put himself in a state of war with me, and whether I may, as *Jephtha* did, appeal to Heaven in it? Of that I myself can only be judge in my own conscience, as I will answer it at the great day, to the supreme Judge of all men.

IV
Of Slavery

22. The *natural liberty* of man is to be free from any superior power on earth, and not to be under the will or legislative authority of man, but to have only the law of nature for his rule. The *liberty of man, in society*, is to be under no other legislative power, but that established, by consent, in the commonwealth, nor under the dominion of any will, or restraint of any law, but what the legislative shall enact according to the trust put in it. *Freedom* then is not what Sir Robert Filmer tells us, *O.A.* 55.[1] *A liberty for every one to do what he lists, to live as he pleases, and not to be tied by any laws:* but *freedom of men under government*, is, to have a standing rule to live by, common to every one of that society, and made by the legislative power erected in it; a liberty to follow my own will in all things where the rule prescribes not, not to be subject to the inconstant, uncertain, unknown, arbitrary will of another man. As *freedom of nature* is to be under no other restraint but the law of nature.

23. This *freedom* from absolute, arbitrary power, is so necessary to, and closely joined with, a man's preservation, that he cannot part with it, but by what forfeits his preservation and life together. For a man, not having the power of his own life, *cannot*, by compact, or his own consent, *enslave himself* to any one, nor put himself under the absolute, arbitrary power of another to take away his life, when he pleases. No body can give more power than he has himself; and he that cannot take away his own life cannot give

[1]**Filmer . . . *O.A.* 55:** The passage quoted—the only direct quotation from Filmer in the *Second Treatise*—is from Filmer's *Observations on Aristotle's Politics*.

another power over it. Indeed, having, by his fault, forfeited his own life, by some act that deserves death; he, to whom he has forfeited it may (when he has him in his power) delay to take it, and make use of him to his own service, and he does him no injury by it. For, whenever he finds the hardship of his slavery outweigh the value of his life, 'tis in his power, by resisting the will of his master, to draw on himself the death he desires.

24. This is the perfect condition of *slavery,*[2] which *is* nothing else but *the state of war continued between a lawful conqueror and a captive.* For, if once *compact* enter between them, and make an agreement for a limited power on the one side, and obedience on the other, the state of war and *slavery* ceases, as long as the compact endures. For, as has been said, no man can by agreement pass over to another that which he hath not in himself, a power over his own life.

I confess, we find among the *Jews,* as well as other nations, that men did sell themselves; but 'tis plain this was only to *drudgery, not to slavery.* For, it is evident, the person sold was not under an absolute, arbitrary, despotical power. For the master could not have power to kill him, at any time, whom, at a certain time, he was obliged to let go free out of his service: and the master of such a servant was so far from having an arbitrary power over his life, that he could not, at pleasure, so much as maim him, but the loss of an eye, or tooth, set him free, *Exod. xxi.*

[2]**perfect condition of *slavery:*** Locke was well aware that in one of the most important ancient writings on slavery—Aristotle, *Politics,* Book I—it is argued that *some* men are "by nature" fit to be slaves, and others "by nature" to be masters. Locke's doctrine flatly opposes Aristotle's. Note that Locke's discussion of "property" immediately follows his discussion of "slavery": Locke *excludes* "slaves" from "property," whereas Aristotle had argued that slaves are the most important *kind* of property.

V

Of Property

25. Whether we consider natural *reason*, which tells us, that men, being once born, have a right to their preservation, and consequently to meat and drink, and such other things, as nature affords for their subsistence: Or *Revelation*,[1] which gives us an account of those grants God made of the world to *Adam*, and to *Noah* and his sons, 'tis very clear that God, as King *David* says, *Psalm cxv. 16, has given the earth to the children of men*, given it to mankind in common. But this being supposed, it seems to some a very great difficulty, how any one should ever come to have a *property* in anything: I will not content myself to answer, that if it be difficult to make out *property*, upon a supposition that God gave the world to *Adam* and his posterity in common; it is impossible that any man, but one universal monarch, should have any *property*, upon a supposition that God gave the world to *Adam* and his heirs in succession, exclusive of all the rest of his posterity. But I shall endeavour to shew, how men might come to have a *property* in several parts of that which God gave to mankind in common, and that without any express compact of all the commoners.

26. God, who hath given the world to men in common, hath also given them reason to make use of it to the best advantage of life, and convenience. The earth, and all that is therein, is given to men for the support and comfort of

[1]***reason . . . Revelation:*** Whether "revelation" and Locke's kind of "reasoning" teach the same thing concerning the nature of "property" is a crucial question. It is worth noting, for example, in considering this question, that Locke frequently refers to revelation, to God, and to the Bible, in the first half of the chapter; but he is wholly silent about them in the second half.

h all the fruits it naturally produces, ıg to mankind in common, as they ıtaneous hand of nature; and no ate dominion, exclusive of the them, as they are thus in their ven for the use of men, there eans *to appropriate* them some way y can be of any use, or at all beneficial ular man. The fruit, or venison, which the wild *Indian,* who knows no enclosure, and is a tenant in common, must be his, and so his *i.e.,* a part of him, that another can no longer have any right to it, before it can do him any good for the support of his life.

27. Though the earth, and all inferior creatures be common to all men, yet every man has a *property* in his own *person.* This no body has any right to but himself. The *labour*[2] of his body, and the *work* of his hands, we may say, are properly his. Whatsoever then he removes out of the state that nature hath provided, and left it in, he hath mixed his *labour* with and joined to it something that is his own, and thereby makes it his property. It being by him removed from the common state nature placed it in, it hath by this *labour* something annexed to it, that excludes the common right of other men. For this *labour* being the unquestionable property of the labourer, no man but he can have a right to what that is once joined to, at least where there is enough, and as good left in common for others.

[2]***Labour:*** Locke's argument concerning the character of human "labor," and its relationships to "natural" things—such as wild plants, or virgin soil, or fish in the sea—is one of the most important bases of the whole modern doctrine of the "labor theory of value." It is helpful in studying this chapter to read the article on "labor" in the *Oxford English Dictionary*. Thus, one finds that the noun comes from the Latin *laborem,* labor, toil, distress, trouble. The first *O.E.D.* definition very aptly catches the sense of what Locke is driving at: "Exertion of the faculties of the body or mind, *especially when painful or compulsory*. . ." (emphasis supplied). Natural things generally require a great expenditure of labor in order to become of any real *use* to humans, Locke will argue as the chapter progresses. What then becomes of the original image, in Section 25, of a bountiful, God-given world of natural things?

28. He that is nourished by the acorns he picked up under an oak, or the apples he gathered from the trees in the wood, has certainly appropriated them to himself. No body can deny but the nourishment is his. I ask then, When did they begin to be his? When he digested? Or when he ate? Or when he boiled? Or when he brought them home? Or when he picked them up? And 'tis plain, if the first gathering made them not his, nothing else could. That *labour* put a distinction between them and common. That added something to them more than nature, the common mother of all, had done; and so they became his private right. And will any one say he had no right to those acorns or apples he thus approriated, because he had not the consent of all mankind to make them his? Was it a robbery thus to assume to himself what belonged to all in common? If such a consent as that was necessary, man had starved, notwithstanding the plenty God had given him. We see in *commons,* which remain so by compact, that 'tis the taking any part of what is common, and removing it out of the state nature leaves it in, which *begins the property* without which the common is of no use. And the taking of this or that part does not depend on the express consent of all the commoners. Thus the grass my horse has bit; the turfs my servant has cut; and the ore I have digged in any place, where I have a right to them in common with others, become my *property* without the assignation or consent of any body. The *labour* that was mine, removing them out of that common state they were in, hath *fixed* my *property* in them.

29. By making an explicit consent of every commoner, necessary to any one's appropriating to himself any part of what is given in common, children or servants could not cut the meat which their father or master had provided for them in common, without assigning to every one his peculiar part. Though the water running in the fountain be every one's, yet who can doubt, but that in the pitcher is his only who drew it out? His *labour* hath taken it out of the hands of nature where it was common, and belonged equally to all her children, and *hath* thereby *appropriated* it to himself.

30. Thus this law of reason makes the deer that *Indian's* who hath killed it; 'tis allowed to be his goods who hath bestowed his labour upon it, though before, it was the com-

mon right of every one. And amongst those who are counted the civilized part of mankind, who have made and multiplied positive laws to determine property, this original law of nature for the *beginning of property,* in what was before common, still takes place; and by virtue thereof, what fish any one catches in the ocean, that great and still remaining common of mankind; or what ambergris any one takes up here, is *by* the *labour* that removes it out of that common state nature left it in, *made* his *property* who takes that pains about it. And even amongst us the hare that any one is hunting is thought his who pursues her during the chase. For being a beast that is still looked upon as common, and no man's private possession; whoever has employed so much *labour* about any of that kind as to find and pursue her, has thereby removed her from the state of nature, wherein she was common, and hath *begun a property.*

31. It will perhaps be objected to this, That if gathering the acorns or other fruits of the earth, etc., makes a right to them, then any one day may *engross* as much as he will. To which I answer, Not so. The same law of nature, that does by this means give us property, does also *bound* that *property* too. *God has given us all things richly,* 1 *Tim.* vi. 12. [*sic*][3] Is the voice of reason confirmed by inspiration. But how far has he given it us? *To enjoy.* As much as any one can make use of to any advantage of life before it spoils; so much he may by his labour fix a property in. Whatever is beyond this, is more than his share, and belongs to others. Nothing was made by God for man to spoil or destroy. And thus considering the plenty of natural provisions there was a long time in the world, and the few spenders, and to how small a part of that provision the industry of one man could extend itself, and engross it to the prejudice of others, especially keeping within the *bonds,* set by reason of what might serve for his *use;* there could be

[3]***God has given . . .:*** the reader should restore the passage from I. *Timothy* 6:17 to its original context, and watch closely how Locke profoundly transforms—or even repudiates—the biblical teaching, while appearing only to cite it as "authority."

then little room for quarrels or contentions about property so established.

32. But the *chief matter of property* being now not the fruits of the earth, and the beasts that subsist on it, but the *earth it self;* as that which takes in and carries with it all the rest: I think it is plain, that *property* in that too is acquired as the former. *As much land* as a man tills, plants, improves, cultivates, and can use the product of, so much is his *property.* He by his labour does, as it were, enclose it from the common. Nor will it invalidate his right to say, Every body else has an equal title to it, and therefore he cannot appropriate, he cannot enclose, without the consent of all his fellow-commoners, all mankind. God, when he gave the world in common to all mankind, commanded man also to labour, and the penury of his condition required it of him. God and his reason commanded him to subdue the earth, i.e., improve it for the benefit of life, and therein lay out something upon it that was his own, his labour. He that in obedience to this command of God, subdued, tilled, and sowed any part of it, thereby annexed to it something that was his *property,* which another had no title to, nor could without injury take from him.

33. Nor was this *appropriation* of any parcel of *land,* by improving it, any prejudice to any other man since there was still enough, and as good left; and more than the yet unprovided could use. So that in effect, there was never the less left for others because of his enclosure for himself. For he that leaves as much as another can make use of, does as good as take nothing at all. No body could think himself injured by the drinking of another man, though he took a good draught, who had a whole river of the same water left him to quench his thirst. And the case of land and water, where there is enough of both, is perfectly the same.

34. God gave the world to men in common; but since he gave it them for their benefit and the greatest conveniences of life they were capable to draw from it, it cannot be supposed he meant it should always remain common and uncultivated. He gave it to the use of the industrious and rational (and *labour* was to be *his title* to it); not to the fancy or covetousness of the quarrelsome and contentious. He that had as good left for his improvement, as was already

taken up needed not complain, ought not to meddle with what was already improved by another's labour: if he did, 'tis plain he desired the benefit of another's pains, which he had no right to, and not the ground which God had given him, in common with others, to labour on, and whereof there was as good left, as that already possessed, and more than he knew what to do with, or his industry could reach to.

35. 'Tis true, in *land* that is *common* in *England* or any other country, where there are plenty of people under government, who have money and commerce, no one can enclose or appropriate any part without the consent of all his fellow commoners: because this is left common by compact, i.e., by the law of the land, which is not to be violated. And though it be common, in respect of some men, it is not so to all mankind; but is the joint property of this country, or this parish. Besides, the remainer, after such enclosure, would not be as good to the rest of the commoners as the whole was, when they could all make use of the whole: whereas in the beginning and and first peopling of the great common of the world, it was quite otherwise. The law man was under, was rather for *appropriating*. God commanded, and his wants forced him to *labour*. That was his *property* which could not be taken from him wherever he had fixed it. And hence subduing or cultivating the earth, and having dominion, we see are joined together. The one gave title to the other. So that God, by commanding to subdue, gave authority so far to *appropriate*. And the condition of human life, which requires labour and materials to work on, necessarily introduce[s] *private possessions*.

36. The measure of property nature has well set, by the extent of men's *labour* and the *conveniency of life:* No man's labour could subdue, or appropriate all: nor could his enjoyment consume more than a small part; so that it was impossible for any man, this way, to entrench upon the right of another, or acquire, to himself, a property, to the prejudice of his neighbour, who would still have room for as good, and as large a possession (after the other had taken out his) as before it was appropriated. This *measure* did confine every man's *possession* to a very moderate proportion, and such as he might appropriate to himself, without injury to any body, in the first ages of the world, when men

were more in danger to be lost, by wandering from their company, in the then vast wilderness of the earth, than to be straitened for want of room to plant in. And the same *measure* may be allowed still, without prejudice to any body, as full as the world seems. For, supposing a man, or family, in the state they were at first peopling of the world by the children of *Adam* or *Noah;* let him plant in some inland, vacant places of *America,* we shall find that the *possessions* he could make himself upon the measures we have given, would not be very large, nor, even to this day, prejudice the rest of mankind or give them reason to complain, or think themselves injured by this man's encroachment, though the race of men have now spread themselves to all corners of the world, and do infinitely exceed the small number [which] was at the beginning. Nay, the extent of *ground* is of so little value, *without labour* that I have heard it affirmed, that in *Spain* itself, a man may be permitted to plough, sow, and reap, without being disturbed, upon land he has no other title to, but only his making use of it. But, on the contrary, the inhabitants think themselves beholden to him, who, by his industry on neglected, and consequently waste land, has increased the stock of corn, which they wanted. But be this as it will, which I lay no stress; this I dare boldly affirm, that the same *rule of propriety* (*viz.*), that every man should have as much as he could make use of, would hold still in the world, without straitening any body, since there is land enough in the world to suffice double the inhabitants had not the *invention of money,* and the tacit agreement of men to put a value on it, introduced (by consent) larger possessions, and a right to them; which, how it has done, I shall, by and by, show more at large.

37. This is certain, that in the beginning, before the desire of having more than man needed, had altered the intrinsic value of things, which depends only on their usefulness to the life of man; or had *agreed that a little piece of yellow metal,* which would keep without wasting or decay, should be worth a great piece of flesh, or a whole heap of corn, though men had a right to appropriate by their labour, each one to himself, as much of the things of nature as he could use, yet this could not be much, nor to the prejudice of others, where the same plenty was still left, to those who would use the same industry. To which let me

add, that he who appropriates land to himself by his labor does not lessen but increases the common stock of mankind. For the provisions serving to the support of human life produced by one acre of enclosed and cultivated land, are (to speak much within compass) ten times more, than those which are yielded by an acre of land of an equal richness, lying waste in common. And therefore he that encloses land, and has a greater plenty of the conveniences of life from ten acres than he could have from an hundred left to nature, may truly be said to give ninety acres to mankind. For his labor now supplies him with provisions out of ten acres, which were but the product of an hundred lying in common. I have here rated the improved land very low in making its product but as ten to one, when it is much nearer an hundred to one. For I ask whether in the wild woods and uncultivated waste of America left to nature, without any improvement, tillage or husbandry, a thousand acres yield the needy and wretched inhabitants as many conveniences of life as ten acres of equally fertile land do in Devonshire where they are well cultivated?[4]

Before the appropriation of land, he who gathered as much of the wild fruit, killed, caught, or tamed as many of the beasts as he could; he that so employed his pains about any of the spontaneous products of nature, as any way to alter them, from the state which nature put them in, *by* placing any of his *labour* on them, did thereby *acquire a propriety in them:* But if they perished, in his possession without their due use; if the fruits rotted, or the venison putrified, before he could spend it, he offended against the common law of nature, and was liable to be punished; he invaded his neighbour's share, for he had *no right, far-*

[4]**To which . . . cultivated?** Locke added this passage in the Christ's College copy. Note that Locke first computes the ratio of what human labor adds to natural things at a hefty 10–1, but then, tentatively, suggests it is "much nearer" to 100–1. Three sections later (Section 40), Locke drops the equivocation: It is now a ratio of 100–1. And three sections later still, the ratio jumps tenfold, to 1000–1. The value of what nature—or God?—has given mankind directly for their use thus declines precipitously as the chapter progresses. See my remarks in the Introduction about Locke's project of making men more at home in this world by making them masters of it.

ther than his use called for any of them, and they might serve to afford him conveniencies of life.

38. The same *measures* governed the *possession of land, too:* Whatsoever he tilled and reaped, laid up and made use of, before it spoiled, that was his peculiar right; whatsoever he enclosed, and could feed and make use of, the cattle and product was also his. But if either the grass of his enclosure rotted on the ground, or the fruit of his planting perished without gathering, and laying up, this part of the earth, notwithstanding his enclosure was still to be looked on as waste, and might be the possession of any other. Thus, at the beginning, *Cain* might take as much ground as he could till, and make it his own land, and yet leave enough to *Abel's* sheep to feed on; a few acres would serve for both their possessions. But as families increased, and industry enlarged their stocks, their *possessions enlarged* with the need of them; but yet it was commonly *without any fixed property in the ground* they made use of, till they incorporated, settled themselves together, and built cities, and then, by consent, they came in time to set out the *bounds of their distinct territories,* and agree on limits between them and their neighbours, and by laws within themselves, settled the *properties* of those of the same society. For we see, that in that part of the world which was first inhabited, and therefore like to be best peopled, even as low down as *Abraham's* time, they wandered with their flocks and their herds, which was their substance, freely up and down; and this *Abraham* did, in a country where he was a stranger. Whence it is plain, that at least, a great part of the *land lay in common;* that the inhabitants valued it not, nor claimed property in any more than they made use of. But when there was not room enough in the same place, for their herds to feed together, they, by consent, as Abraham and Lot did, *Gen.* xiii. 5, separated and enlarged their pasture, where it best liked them. And for the same reason, *Esau* went from his father, and his brother, and planted in *Mount Seir, Gen.* xxxvi. 6.

39. And thus, without supposing any private dominion, and property in *Adam,* over all the world, exclusive of all other men, which can no way be proved, nor any one's property be made out from it; but supposing the *world* given as it was to the children of men *in common,* we see how

labour could make men distinct titles to several parcels of it, for their private uses; wherein there could be no doubt of right, no room for quarrel.

40. Nor is it so strange, as perhaps before consideration it may appear, that the *property of labour* should be able to overbalance the community of land. For 'tis *labour* indeed that *puts the difference* of value on every thing; and let any one consider, what the difference is between an acre of land planted with tobacco or sugar, sown with wheat or barley; and an acre of the same land lying in common, without any husbandry upon it, and he will find that the improvement of *labour makes* the far greater part of *the value.* I think it will be but a very modest computation to say, that of the *products* of the earth useful to the life of man, nine-tenths are the *effects of labour:* nay, if we will rightly estimate things as they come to our use, and cast up the several expenses about them, what in them is purely owing to *nature, and what to labour,* we shall find that in most of them ninety-nine hundredths are wholly to be put on the account of *labour.*

41. There cannot be a clearer demonstration of any thing, than several nations of the *Americans* are of this, who are rich in land and poor in all the comforts of life; whom nature having furnished as liberally as any other people, with the materials of plenty, i.e., a fruitful soil, apt to produce in abundance, what might serve for food, raiment, and delight; yet for want of improving it by labour, have not one hundredth part of the conveniencies we enjoy: And a king of a large and fruitful territory there feeds, lodges, and is clad worse than a day labourer in *England.*

42. To make this a little clearer, let us but trace some of the ordinary provisions of life, through their several progresses, before they come to our use, and see how much they receive of their *value from human industry.* Bread, wine, and cloth are things of daily use, and great plenty, yet notwithstanding, acorns, water, and leaves, or skins must be our bread, drink and clothing, did not *labour* furnish us with these more useful commodities. For whatever *bread* is more worth than acorns, *wine* than water, and *cloth* or *silk* than leaves, skins or moss, that is wholly *owing to labour* and industry. The one of these being the food and raiment which unassisted nature furnishes us with; the other provi-

sions which our industry and pains prepare for us, which how much they exceed the other in value, when any one hath computed, he will then see, how much *labour makes the far greatest part of the value* of things, we enjoy in this world: and the ground which produces the materials, is scarce to be reckoned in, as any, or at most, but a very small part of it; so little, that even amongst us, land that is left wholly to nature, that hath no improvement of pasturage, tillage, or planting, is called, as indeed it is, waste; and we shall find the benefit of it amount to little more than nothing. This shows, how much numbers of men are to be preferred to largeness of dominions, and that the increase of lands and the right employing of them is the great art of government. And that prince who shall be so wise and godlike as by established laws of liberty to secure protection and encouragement to the honest industry of mankind against the oppression of power and narrowness of party will quickly be too hard for his neighbors. But this by the by. To return to the argument in hand.[5]

43. An acre of land that bears here twenty bushels of wheat, and another in *America,* which, with the same husbandry, would do the like, are, without doubt, of the same natural, intrinsic value. But yet the benefit mankind receives from the one in a year, is worth five pounds, and, from the other possibly not worth a penny, if all the profit an *Indian* received from it were to be valued and sold here; at least, I may truly say, not one thousandth. 'Tis *labor* then which *puts the greatest part of value upon land,* without which it would scarcely be worth any thing: 'tis to that we owe the greatest part of all its useful products: for all that the straw, bran, bread, of that acre of wheat, is more worth than the product of an acre of as good land, which lies waste, is all the effect of labour. For 'tis not barely the

[5]**This shows. . .hand:** Locke added this passage in the Christ's College copy. It is one of the rare places where he uses the words "wise" and "godlike" to refer to human rulers. All the more notable, then, is the object Locke here prescribes to such rulers: to protect and encourage the "honest industry of mankind." Such industry is meant to transform the world of natural scarcity into a new world of abundance produced by humans. (See another use of such language, regarding "prerogative," II. 166.)

ploughman's pains, the reaper's and thresher's toil, and the baker's sweat, is to be counted into the bread we eat; the labour of those who broke the oxen, who digged and wrought the iron and stones, who felled and framed the timber employed about the plough, mill, oven, or any other utensils, which are a vast number, requisite to this corn, from its being seed to be sown to its being made bread, must all be *charged* on the account of *labour,* and received as an effect of that: nature and the earth furnished only the almost worthless materials, as in themselves. 'Twould be a strange *catalogue of things, that industry provided and made use of, about every loaf of bread,* before it came to our use, if we could trace them; iron, wood, leather, bark, timber, stone, bricks, coals, lime, cloth, dyeing-drugs, pitch, tar, masts, ropes, and all the materials made use of in the ship, that brought any of the commodities made use of by any of the workmen, to any part of the work, all which, 'twould be almost impossible, at least too long, to reckon up.

44. From all which it is evident, that though the things of nature are given in common, yet man (by being master of himself, and *proprietor of his own person,* and the actions or *labour* of it) had still in himself the *great foundation of property;* and that which made up the great part of what he applied to the support or comfort of his being, when invention and arts had improved the conveniencies of life, was perfectly his own, and did not belong in common to others.

45. Thus *labour,* in the beginning, *gave a right of property,* wherever any one was pleased to employ it, upon what was common, which remained, a long while, the far greater part, and is yet more than mankind makes use of. Men, at first, for the most part, contented themselves with what unassisted nature offered to their necessities: and though afterwards, in some parts of the world, (where the increase of people and stock, with the *use of money*) had made land scarce, and so of some value, the several *communities* settled the bounds of their distinct territories, and by laws within themselves, regulated the properties of the private men of their society, and so, *by compact* and agreement, *settled the property* which labour and industry began; and the leagues that have been made between several states and kingdoms,

either expressly or tacitly disowning all claim and right to the land in the other's possession, have, by common consent, given up their pretences to their natural common right, which originally they had to those countries, and so have, by *positive agreement, settled a property* amongst themselves, in distinct parcels of the earth: yet there are still *great tracts of ground* to be found, which (the inhabitants thereof not having joined with the rest of mankind in the consent of the use of their common money) *lie waste,* and are more than the people who dwell on it, do, or can make use of, and so still lie in common. Though this can scarce happen amongst that part of mankind that have consented to the use of money.

46. The greatest part of *things really useful* to the life of man, and such as the necessity of subsisting made the first commoners of the world look after, as it doth the *Americans* now, *are* generally things *of short duration;* such as, if they are not consumed by use, will decay and perish of themselves: Gold, silver, and diamonds, are things that fancy or agreement hath put the value on, more than real use, and the necessary support of life. Now of those good things which nature hath provided in common, every one had a right (as hath been said) to as much as he could use, and had a property in all that he could effect with his labour: all that his industry could extend to, to alter from the state nature had put it in, was his. He that *gathered* a hundred bushels of acorns or apples, had thereby a *property* in them; they were his goods as soon as gathered. He was only to look that he used them before they spoiled, else he took more than his share, and robbed others. And indeed it was a foolish thing, as well as dishonest, to hoard up more than he could make use of. If he gave away a part to any body else, so that it perished not uselessly in his possession, these he also made use of. And if he also bartered away plums that would have rotted in a week, for nuts that would last good for his eating a whole year, he did no injury; he wasted not the common stock; destroyed no part of the portion of goods that belonged to others, so long as nothing perished uselessly in his hands. Again, if he would give his nuts for a piece of metal, pleased with its colour; or exchange his sheep for shells, or wool for a sparkling pebble or a diamond, and keep those by him all his life, he invad-

ed not the right of others, he might heap up as much of these durable things as he pleased; the *exceeding of the bounds of his* just *property* not lying in the largeness of his possession, but the perishing of anything uselessly in it.

47. And thus *came in the use of money,* some lasting thing that men might keep without spoiling, and that by mutual consent, men would take in exchange for the truly useful, but perishable supports of life.

48. And as different degrees of industry were apt to give men possessions in different proportions, so this *invention of money* gave them the opportunity to continue and enlarge them. For supposing an island, separate from all possible commerce with the rest of the world, wherein there were but a hundred families, but there were sheep, horses and cows, with other useful animals, wholesome fruits, and land enough for corn for a hundred thousand times as many, but nothing in the island, either because of its commonness or perishableness, fit to supply the place of *money:* What reason could any one have there to enlarge his possessions beyond the use of his family, and a plentiful supply to its consumption, either in what their own industry produced, or they could barter for like perishable, useful commodities with others? Where there is not something both lasting and scarce, and so valuable to be hoarded up, there men will not be apt to enlarge their *possessions of land,* were it never so rich, never so free for them to take. For I ask, what would a man value ten thousand or an hundred thousand acres of excellent *land,* ready cultivated, and well stocked too, with cattle, in the middle of the inland parts of *America,* where he had no hopes of commerce with other parts of the world, to draw *money* to him by the sale of the product? It would not be worth the enclosing, and we should see him give up again to the wild common of nature, whatever was more than would supply the conveniencies of life, to be had there for him and his family.

49. Thus, in the beginning, all the world was *America,* and more so than that is now; for no such thing as *money* was any where known. Find out something that hath the *use and value of money* amongst his neighbours, you shall see the same man will begin presently to *enlarge* his *possessions.*

50. But since gold and silver, being little useful to the life of man in proportion to food, raiment, and carriage,

has its *value* only from the consent of men, whereof labour yet makes in great part *the measure,* it is plain that men have agreed to disproportionate and unequal possession of the earth, they having by a tacit and voluntary consent found out a way, how a man may possess fairly more land than he himself can use, of the product; by receiving in exchange for the overplus, gold and silver, which may be hoarded up without injury to any one, these metals not spoiling or decaying in hands of the possessors. This partage of things, in an inequality of private possessions, men have made practicable out of society, and without compact, only by putting a value on gold and silver and tacitly agreeing in the use of money. For in governments the laws regulate the right of property, and the possession of land is determined by positive constitutions.[6]

51. And thus, I think, it is very easy to conceive, without any difficulty, *how labour could at first begin a title of property* in the common things of nature, and how the spending it upon our uses bounded it. So that there could then be no reason of quarrelling about title, nor any doubt about the largeness of possession it gave. Right and conveniency went together; for as a man had a right to all he could employ his labour upon, so he had no temptation to labour for more than he could make use of. This left no room for controversy about the title, nor for encroachment on the right of others; What portion a man carved to himself was easily seen; and it was useless as well as dishonest to carve himself too much, or take more than he needed.

[6]**it is plain . . .constitutions:** Locke modified and added to this section in the Christ's College copy. It is difficult to be sure, in two places, exactly how the additions should read. An alternative reading to that given in the text would be: ". . . how a man may fairly possess more land than he himself can use the product of, by receiving. . . ." Note particularly the *justification* of "hoarding up" gold and silver, "out of the bounds of society" and "without compact," simply on the basis of a "tacit and voluntary consent" among men to use "money." What has become of the Christian teaching against heaping up—let alone hoarding—the things of *this* world?

VI

Of Paternal Power

52. It may perhaps be censured as an impertinent criticism in a discourse of this nature, to find fault with words and names that have obtained in the world: And yet possibly it may not be amiss to offer new ones when the old are apt to lead men into mistakes, as this of *paternal power* probably has done, which seems so to place the power of parents over their children wholly in the *father,* as if the *mother* had no share in it, whereas if we consult reason or revelation, we shall find she hath an equal title. This may give one reason to ask, Whether this might not be more properly called *parental power.* For whatever obligation nature and the right of generation lays on children, it must certainly bind them equal to both the concurrent causes of it. And accordingly we see the positive law of God every where joins them together, without distinction, when it commands the obedience of children, *Honour they father and thy mother, Exod. xx..12. Whosoever curseth his father or his mother, Lev.* xx. 9. *Ye shall fear every man his mother and his father, Lev.* xix. 3. *Children, obey your parents, Eph.* etc. vi. 1. is the style of the Old and New Testament.

53. Had but this one thing been well considered without looking any deeper into the matter, it might perhaps have kept men from running into those gross mistakes, they have made, about this power of parents: which however, it might, without any great harshness, bear the name of absolute dominion, and regal authority, when under the title of *paternal power* it seemed appropriated to the father, would yet have sounded but oddly, and in the very name shown the absurdity, if this supposed absolute power over children had been called *parental,* and thereby have discovered that it belonged to the *mother* too; for it will but very ill serve the turn of those men who contend so much for the

absolute power and authority of the *fatherhood, as they call it, that the mother* should have any share in it. And it would have but ill supported the *monarchy* they contend for, when by the very name it appeared that the fundamental authority from whence they would derive their government of a single person only, was not placed in one, but two persons jointly. But to let this of names pass.

54. Though I have said above (*Chap.* 2.) *That all men by nature are equal,* I cannot be supposed to understand all sorts of *equality:*[1] *Age* or *virtue* may give men a just precedency: *Excellency of parts and merit* may place others above the common level: *Birth* may subject some, and *alliance* or *benefits* others, to pay an observance to those to whom nature, gratitude, or other respects may have made it due; and yet all this consists with the *equality,* which all men are in in respect of jurisdiction or dominion one over another, which was the *equality* I there spoke of as proper to the business in hand, being that *equal right* that every man hath *to his natural freedom,* without being subjected to the will or authority of any other man.

55. *Children,* I confess are not born in this full state of *equality,* though they are born to it. Their parents have a sort of rule and jurisdiction over them when they come into the world, and for some time after, but 'tis but a temporary one. The bonds of this subjection are like the swaddling clothes they are wrapt up in, and supported by in the weakness of their infancy. Age and reason as they grow up, loosen them till at length they drop quite off, and leave a man at his own free disposal.

56. *Adam* was created a perfect man, his body and mind in full possession of their strength and reason, and so was capable from the first instant of his being to provide for his own support and preservation, and govern his actions according to the dictates of the law of reason which God had implanted in him. From him the world is peopled with his descendants, who are all born infants, weak and helpless, without knowledge or understanding. But to supply the

[1]**I cannot . . . all sorts of *equality:*** the carefully limited sense of natural equality articulated in this section is also present in the Declaration of Independence.

defects of this imperfect state, till the improvement of growth and age had removed them, *Adam* and *Eve,* and after them all *parents* were by the law of nature, *under an obligation to preserve, nourish, and educate the children* they had begotten, not as their own workmanship, but the workmanship of their own Maker, the Almighty, to whom they were to be accountable for them.

57. The law that was to govern *Adam,* was the same that was to govern all his posterity, the *law of reason.* But his offspring having another way of entrance into the world, different from him, by a natural birth, that produced them ignorant, and without the use of *reason,* they were not presently *under that law:* for no body can be under a law which is not promulgated to him, and this law being promulgated or made known by *reason* only, he that is not come to the use of his reason cannot, be said to be *under this law; and Adam's* children being not presently as soon as born, *under this law of reason* were not presently *free.* For *law,* in its true notion, is not so much the limitation as the direction of *a free and intelligent agent* to his proper interest, and prescribes no farther than is for the general good of those under that law. Could they be happier without it, the *law,* as a useless thing would of itself vanish, and that ill deserves the name of confinement which hedges us in only from bogs and precipices. So that, however it may be mistaken, *the end of law* is not to abolish or restrain, but *to preserve and enlarge freedom:* For in all the states of created beings capable of laws, *where there is no law, there is no freedom.* For *liberty* is to be free from restraint and violence from others which cannot be where there is no law: But freedom is not, as we are told, *A liberty for every man to do what he lists:* (For who could be free, when every other man's humour might domineer over him?) But a *liberty* to dispose, and order, freely as he lists, his person, actions, possessions, and his whole property, within the allowance of those laws under which he is; and therein not to be subject to the aribtrary will of another, but freely follow his own.

58. The *power,* then, *that parents have* over their children, arises from that duty which is incumbent on them, to take care of their offspring during the imperfect state of childhood. To inform the mind, and govern the actions of their

yet ignorant nonage, till reason shall take its place and ease them of that trouble, is what the children want, and the parents are bound to. For God having given man an understanding to direct his actions, has allowed him a freedom of will, and liberty of acting, as properly belonging thereunto, within the bounds of that law he is under. But whilst he is in an estate, wherein he has no *understanding* of his own to direct his *will,* he is not to have any will of his own to follow: He that *understands* for him, must *will* for him too, he must prescribe to his will, and regulate his actions; but when he comes to the estate that made his *father a freeman,* the *son is a freeman* too.

59. This holds in all the laws a man is under, whether natural or civil. Is a man under the law of nature? *What made him free* of that law? What gave him a free disposing of his property, according to his own will, within the compass of that law? I answer; State of maturity wherein he might be supposed capable to know that law, that so he might keep his actions within the bounds of it. When he has acquired that state, he is presumed to know how far that law is to be his guide, and how far he may make use of his *freedom,* and so comes to have it; till then, some body else must guide him, who is presumed to know how far the law allows a liberty. If such a state of reason, such an age of discretion *made him free,* the same shall make his son free too. Is a man under the law of *England? What made him free* of that law? That is, to have the liberty to dispose of his actions and possessions, according to his own will, within the permission of that law? A capacity of knowing that law. Which is supposed, by that law, at the age of one and twenty years, and in some cases sooner. If this *made* the father *free,* it shall *make* the son *free* too. Till then we see the law allows the son to have no will, but he is to be guided by the will of his father or guardian, who is to understand for him. And if the father die, and fail to substitute a deputy in this trust, if he hath not provided a tutor to govern his son during his minority, during his want of understanding, the law takes care to do it, some other must govern him and be a will to him till he hath *attained to a state of freedom,* and his understanding be fit to take the government of his will. But after that, the father and son are equally *free* as much as tutor and pupil after nonage; equally subjects of the

same law together, without any dominion left in the father over the life, liberty, or estate of his son, whether they be only in the state and under the law of nature, or under the positive laws of an established government.

60. But if through defects that may happen out of the ordinary course of nature, anyone comes not to such a degree of reason wherein he might be supposed capable of knowing the law, and so living within the rules of it, he is *never capable of being a free man,* he is never let loose to the disposure of his own will (because he knows no bounds to it, has not understanding, its proper guide) but is continued under the tuition and government of others, all the time his own understanding is incapable of that charge. And so *lunatics* and *idiots* are never set free from the government of their parents; *Children, who are not as yet come unto those years whereat they may have; and innocents, which are excluded by a natural defect from ever having;* Thirdly, *Madmen, which, for the present, cannot possibly have the use of right reason to guide themselves, have for their guide, the reason that guideth other men which are tutors over them, to seek and procure their good for them,* says Hooker, *Eccl. Pol.,* lib. i, sect. 7. All which seems no more than that duty, which God and nature has laid on man as well as other creatures, to preserve their offspring till they can be able to shift for themselves, and will scarce amount to an instance or proof of *parents'* regal authority.

61. Thus we are *born free,* as we are born rational; not that we have actually the exercise of either: age that brings one, brings with it the other too. And thus we see how *natural freedom and subjection to parents* may consist together, and are both founded on the same principle. A *child* is *free* by his father's title, by his father's understanding, which is to govern him, till he hath it of his own. The *freedom of a man at years of discretion,* and the *subjection* of a child *to* his *parents,* whilst yet short of that age, are so consistent and so distinguishable, that the most blinded contenders for monarchy, *by right of fatherhood,* cannot miss this *difference,* the most obstinate cannot but allow their consistency. For were their doctrine all true, were the right heir of *Adam* now known, and by that title settled a monarch in his throne, invested with all the absolute, unlimited power Sir Robert Filmer talks of; if he should die as soon as his heir was

born, must not the child, notwithstanding he were never so free, never so much sovereign, be in subjection to his mother and nurse, to tutors and governors, till age and education brought him reason and ability to govern himself, and others? The necessities of his life, the health of his body, and the information of his mind would require him to be directed by the will of others and not his own: and yet will anyone think, that this restraint and subjection were inconsistent with, or spoiled him of that liberty or sovereignty he had a right to, or gave away his empire to those who had the government of his nonage? This government over him only prepared him the better and sooner for it. If any body should ask me, When my son is *of age to be free?* I shall answer, Just when his monarch is of age to govern. *But at what time,* says the judicious Hooker, *Eccl. Pol.,* lib. i, sect. 6, *a man may be said to have attained so far forth the use of reason, as sufficeth to make him capable of those laws whereby he is then bound to guide his actions; this is a great deal more easy for sense to discern, than for anyone by skill and learning to determine.*

62. Commonwealths themselves take notice of, and allow that there is a *time when men* are to *begin to act like free men,* and therefore till that time require not oaths of fealty, or allegiance, or other public owning of, or submission to, the government of their countries.

63. The *freedom* then of man and liberty of acting according to his own will, is *grounded* on his having *reason,* which is able to instruct him in that law he is to govern himself by, and make him know how far he is left to the freedom of his own will. To turn him loose to an unrestrained liberty, before he has reason to guide him, is not the allowing him the privilege of his nature to be free; but to thrust him out amongst brutes, and abandon him to a state as wretched, and as much beneath that of a man, as theirs. This is that which puts the *authority* into the *parents'* hands to govern the *minority* of their children. God hath made it their business to employ this care on their offspring, and hath placed in them suitable inclinations of tenderness and concern to temper this power, to apply it as his wisdom designed it, to the children's good, as long as they should need to be under it.

64. But what reason can hence advance this care of the

parents due to their offspring into an *absolute arbitrary dominion* of the father, whose power reaches no farther, than by such a discipline as he finds most effectual to give such strength and health to their bodies, such vigour and rectitude to their minds, as may best fit his children to be most useful to themselves and others, and, if it be necessary to his condition, to make them work when they are able for their own subsistence. But in his power the *mother* too has her share with the *father*.

65. Nay, this *power* so little belongs to the *father* by any peculiar right of nature, but only as he is guardian of his children, that when he quits his care of them, he loses his power over them, which goes along with their nourishment and education, to which it is inseparably annexed, and it belongs as much to the *foster-father* of an exposed child as to the natural father of another: So little power does the bare *act of begetting* give a man over his issue, if all his care ends there, and this be all the title he hath to the name and authority of a father. And what will become of this *paternal power* in that part of the world where one woman hath more than one husband at a time? Or in those parts of *America* where when husband and wife part, which happens frequently, the children are all left to the mother, follow her, and are wholly under her care and provision? If the father die whilst the children are young, do they not naturally everywhere owe the same obedience to their *mother,* during their minority, as to their father were he alive? And will anyone say, that the *mother* hath a legislative power over her children that she can make standing rules, which shall be of perpetual obligation, by which they ought to regulate all the concerns of their property, and bound their liberty all the course of their lives? Or can she enforce the observation of them with capital punishments? For this is the proper *power of the magistrate,* of which the father hath not so much as the shadow. His command over his children is but temporary, and reaches not their life or property. It is but a help to the weakness and imperfection of their nonage, a discipline necessary to their education; And though a *father* may dispose of his own possessions as he pleases, when his children are out of danger of perishing for want, yet *his power* extends not to the lives or goods, which either their own industry, or another's bounty, has

made theirs; nor to their liberty neither, when they are once arrived to the enfranchisement of the years of discretion. The *father's empire* then ceases, and he can from thence forwards no more dispose of the liberty of his son, than that of any other man: And it must be far from an absolute or perpetual jurisdiction, from which a man may withdraw himself, having licence from Divine authority to *leave father and mother and cleave to his wife.*[2]

66. But though there be a time when a *child* comes to be as *free* from subjection to the will and command of his father, as the father himself is free from subjection to the will of any body else, and they are each under no other restraint but that which is common to them both, whether it be the law of nature, or municipal law of their country: yet this freedom exempts not a son from that *honour* which he ought, by the law of God and nature, *to pay* his *parents.* God having made the parents instruments in his great design of continuing the race of mankind, and the occasions of life to their children, as he hath laid on them an obligation to nourish, preserve, and bring up their offspring; so he has laid on the children a perpetual obligation of *honouring their parents,* which containing in it an inward esteem and reverence to be shown by all outward expressions, ties up the child from anything that may ever injure or affront, disturb, or endanger the happiness or life of those, from whom he received his; and engages him in all actions of defence, relief, assistance, and comfort of those, by whose means he entered into being, and has been made capable of any enjoyments of life. From this obligation no state, no freedom, can absolve children. But this is very far from giving parents a power of command over their children, or an authority to make laws and dispose as they

[2]***leave . . . wife:*** Locke here draws on a passage that originally appears in *Genesis* 2:24, and that is then repeated by Jesus in the New Testament: See *Matthew* 19:5; *Mark* 10:7. The reader should compare this seeming deference to the authority of both Old and New Testament to the *argument* concerning marriage in Chapter VIII, Section 78–83. The argument in Chapter VII is a very important basis for what, in our time, is called the women's liberation movement. Marriage, so far from being a sacrament, is but a "voluntary compact between man and woman" (Section 78).

please of their lives or liberties. 'Tis one thing to owe honour, respect, gratitude, and assistance; another to require an absolute obedience and submission. The *honour due to parents,* a monarch in his throne owes his mother, and yet this lessens not his authority, nor subjects him to her government.

67. The subjection of a minor places in the father a temporary government, which terminates with the minority of the child: and the *honour due from a child,* places in the parents a perpetual right to respect, reverence, support, and compliance too, more or less, as the father's care, cost, and kindness in his education, has been more or less, and this ends not with minority, but holds in all parts and conditions of a man's life. The want of distinguishing these two powers; viz. that which the father hath in the right of *tuition,* during minority, and the right of *honour* all his life, may perhaps have caused a great part of the mistakes about this matter. For to speak properly of them, the first of these is rather the privilege of children, and duty of parents, than any prerogative of paternal power. The nourishment and education of their children, is a charge so incumbent on parents for their children's good, that nothing can absolve them from taking care of it. And though the *power of commanding and chastising* them go along with it, yet God hath woven into the principles of human nature such a tenderness for their offspring, that there is little fear that parents should use their power with too much rigour; the excess is seldom on the severe side, the strong bias of nature drawing the other way. And therefore God Almighty when he would express his gentle dealing with the *Israelites,* he tells them that though he chastened them, *he chastened them as a man chastens his son, Deut.* viii. 5, i.e. with tenderness and affection, and kept them under no severer discipline than what was absolutely best for them, and had been less kindness to have slackened. This is that power to which *children* are commanded *obedience,* that the pains and care of their parents may not be increased, or ill-rewarded.

68. On the other side, *honour* and support, all that which gratitude requires to return for the benefits received by and from them is the indispensable duty of the child, and the proper privilege of the parents. This is intended for

the parents' advantage, as the other is for the child's; though education, the parents' duty, seems to have most power, because the ignorance and infirmities of childhood stand in need of restraint and correction; which is a visible exercise of rule, and a kind of dominion. And that duty which is comprehended in the word *honour,* requires less obedience, though the obligation be stronger on grown than younger children. For who can think the command, *Children obey your parents,* requires in a man that has children of his own the same submission to his father, as it does in his yet young children to him; and that by this precept he were bound to obey all his father's commands, if, out of a conceit of authority, he should have the indiscretion to treat him still as a boy?

69. The first part then of *paternal* power, or rather duty, which is *education,* belongs so to the father that it terminates at a certain season; when the business of education is over it ceases of it self, and is also alienable before. For a man may put the tuition of his son in other hands; and he that has made his son an *apprentice* to another, has discharged him, during that time of a great part of his obedience both to himself and to his mother. But all the *duty of honour,* the other part, remains nevertheless entire to them; nothing can cancel that. It is so inseparable from them both, that the father's authority cannot dispossess the mother of this right, nor can any man discharge his son from *honouring* her that bore him. But both these are very far from a power to make laws, and enforcing them with penalties that may reach estate, liberty, limbs, and life. The power of commanding ends with nonage; and though after that, *honour* and respect, support and defence, and whatsoever gratitude can oblige a man to for the highest benefits he is naturally capable of, be always due from a son to his parents; yet all this puts no sceptre into the father's hand, no sovereign power of commanding. He has no dominion over his son's property or actions, nor any right, that his will should prescribe to his son's in all things; however it may become his son in many things, not very inconvenient to him and his family, to pay a deference to it.

70. A man may owe *honour* and respect to an ancient, or wise man; defence to his child or friend; relief and support

to the distressed; and gratitude to a benefactor, to such a degree, that all he has, all he can do, cannot sufficiently pay it: but all these give no authority, no right to anyone of making laws over him from whom they are owing. And 'tis plain, all this is due not only to the bare title of father, not only because, as has been said, it is owing to the mother too; but because these obligations to parents, and the degrees of what is required of children, may be varied, by the different care and kindness, trouble and expense, which is often employed upon one child more than another.

71. This shows the reason how it comes to pass, that *parents in societies,* where they themselves are subjects, retain a *power over their children* and have as much right to their subjection, as those who are in the state of nature, which could not possibly be, if all political power were only paternal, and that in truth they were one and the same thing: For then, all paternal power being in the prince, the subject could naturally have none of it. But these two *powers, political* and *paternal, are so perfectly distinct* and separate; are built upon so different foundations, and given to so different ends, that every subject that is a father, has as much a *paternal power* over his children, as the prince has over his; and every prince that has parents owes them as much filial duty and obedience as the meanest of his subjects do to theirs; and can therefore contain not any part or degree of that kind of dominion, which a prince, or magistrate has over his subject.

72. Though the obligation on the parents to *bring up* their children, and the obligation on children to *honour* their parents contain all the power on the one hand, and submission on the other, which are proper to this relation: yet there is *another power* ordinarily *in the father,* whereby he has a tie on the obedience of his children: which though it be common to him with other men, yet the occasions of showing it, almost constantly happening to fathers in their private families, and the instances of it elsewhere being rare, and less taken notice of, it passes in the world for a part of *paternal jurisdiction.* And this is the power men generally have to *bestow their estates* on those who please them best. The possession of the father being the expectation and inheritance of the children ordinarily in certain proportions, according to the law and custom of each

country; yet it is commonly in the father's power to bestow it with a more sparing or liberal hand, according as the behavior of this or that child hath comported with his will and humour.

73. This is no small tie[3] on the obedience of children: and there being always annexed to the enjoyment of land, a submission to the government of the country, of which that land is a part; it has been commonly supposed that a *father* could *oblige his posterity to that government,* of which he himself was a subject, and that his compact held them; whereas, it being only a necessary condition annexed to the land, and the inheritance of an estate which is under that government, reaches only those who will take it on that condition, and so is no natural tie or engagement, but a voluntary submission. For *every man's children* being by nature as *free* as himself, or any of his ancestors ever were, may, whilst they are in that freedom, choose what society they will join themselves to, what commonwealth they will put themselves under. But if they will enjoy the *inheritance* of their ancestors, they must take it on the same terms their ancestors had it, and submit to all the conditions annexed to such a possession. By this power indeed fathers oblige their children to obedience to themselves, even when they are past minority, and most commonly too subject them to this or that political power. But neither of these by any peculiar right of *fatherhood,* but by the reward they have in their hands to enforce and recompense such a compliance; and is no more power than what a *French-man* has over an *English-man,* who by the hopes of an estate he will leave him, will certainly have a strong tie on his obedience and if when it is left him, he will enjoy it, he must certainly take it upon the conditions annexed to the *possession of land* in that country where it lies, whether it be *France* or *England.*

74. To conclude then, though the *father's power* of commanding extends no farther than the minority of his chil-

[3]**no small tie:** what in Section 52 was a traditional, biblically based exhortation to "honor thy father" has now become a counsel, rooted in self-interest, to obey one's father *if* one expects to inherit the father's wealth.

dren, and to a degree only fit for the discipline and government of that age: and though that *honour* and respect, and all that which the *Latins* called *piety,* which they indispensably owe to their parents all their lifetimes, and in all estates, with all that support and defence is due[4] to them, gives the father no power of governing, i.e., making laws and exacting penalties on his children; though by all this he has no dominion over the property or actions of his son: yet 'tis obvious to conceive how easy it was in the first ages of the world, and in places still, where the thinness of people gives families leave to separate into unpossessed quarters, and they have room to remove and plant themselves in yet vacant habitations, for the *father of the family* to become the prince of it;* he had been a ruler from the beginning of the infancy of his children: and since without some government it would be hard for them to live together, it was likeliest it should, by the express or tacit consent of the children, when they were grown up, be in the father, where it seemed without any change barely to continue; when indeed nothing more was required to it, than the permitting the *father* to exercise alone in his

[4]**defence is due:** the sense seems to require "which" between "defence" and "due."

*'*It is no improbable opinion, therefore, which the archphilosopher was of, That the chief person in every household was always, as it were, a king: so when numbers of households joined themselves in civil societies together, kings were the first kind of governors amongst them, which is also, as it seemeth, the reason why the name of fathers continued still in them, who, of fathers, were made rulers; as also the ancient custom of governors to do as Melchizedec; and being kings, to exercise the office of priests, which fathers did, at the first, grew, perhaps by the same occasion. Howbeit, this is not the only kind of regiment that has been received in the world. The inconveniences of one kind have caused sundry other to be devised; so that, in a word, all public regiment of what kind soever, seemeth evidently to have risen from the deliberate advice, consultation and composition between men, judging it convenient and behoveful; there being no impossibility in nature, considered by itself, but that man might have lived without any public regiment.*'—Hooker's *Eccl. Pol.*, lib. i, sect. 10.[5]

[5]**It is . . . the archphilosopher:** Hooker uses a traditional phrase, "the archphilosopher," to refer to Aristotle.

family that executive power of the law of nature, which every free man naturally hath, and by that permission resigning up to him a monarchical power, whilst they remained in it. But that this was not by any *paternal right,* but only by the consent of his children, is evident from hence, that nobody doubts but if a stranger, whom chance or business had brought to his family, had there killed any of his children, or committed any other fact, he might condemn and put him to death, or otherwise have punished him as well as any of his children: which was impossible he should do by virtue of any paternal authority over one, who was not his child, but by virtue of that executive power of the law of nature, which as a man he had a right to: and he alone could punish him in his family, where the respect of his children had laid by the exercise of such a power, to give way to the dignity and authority, they were willing should remain in him, above the rest of his family.

75. Thus 'tis easy, and almost natural for children by a tacit, and scarce avoidable consent, to make way for the *father's authority and government.* They had been accustomed in their childhood to follow his direction, and to refer their little differences to him, and when they were men, who fitter to rule them? Their little properties, and less covetousness seldom afforded greater controversies; and when any should arise, where could they have a fitter umpire than he, by whose care they had every one been sustained and brought up, and who had a tenderness for them all? 'Tis no wonder that they made no distinction betwixt minority, and full age; nor looked after one-and-twenty, or any other age, that might make them the free disposers of themselves and fortunes, when they could have no desire to be out of their pupilage. The government they had been under, during it, continued still to be more their protection than restraint: and they could nowhere find a greater security to their peace, liberties, and fortunes than in the *rule of a father.*

76. Thus the natural *fathers of families,* by an insensible change, became the *politic monarchs* of them too: And as they chanced to live long, and leave able, and worthy heirs for several successions, or otherwise; so they laid the foundations of hereditary, or elective kingdoms, under several

constitutions, and manors, according as chance, contrivance, or occasions happened to mould them. But if princes have their titles in the father's right, and it be a sufficient proof of the natural *right of fathers* to political authority, because they commonly were those in whose hands we find, *de facto,* the exercise of government: I say, if this argument be good, it will as strongly prove that all princes, nay princes only, ought to be priests, since 'tis as certain, that in the beginning, *the father of the family was priest, as that he was ruler in his own household.*

VII

Of Political or Civil Society

77. God having made man such a creature that, in his own judgement, it was not good for him to be alone, put him under strong obligations of necessity, convenience, and inclination, to drive him into *society,* as well as fitted him with understanding and language to continue and enjoy it. The *first society* was between man and wife, which gave beginning to that between parents and children; to which, in time, that between master and servant came to be added: And though all these might, and commonly did meet together, and make up but one family, wherein the master or mistress of it had some sort of rule proper to a family; each of these, or all together came short of *political society,* as we shall see, if we consider the different ends, ties, and bounds of each of these.

78. *Conjugal society* is made by a voluntary compact between man and woman: and though it consist chiefly in such a communion and right in one another's bodies, as is necessary to its chief end, procreation; yet it draws with it mutual support, and assistance, and a communion of interest too, as necessary not only to unite their care, and affection; but also necessary to their common offspring, who have a right to be nourished and maintained by them, till they are able to provide for themselves.

79. For the end of *conjunction between male and female,* being not barely procreation, but the continuation of the species, this conjunction betwixt male and female ought to last, even after procreation, so long as is necessary to the nourishment and support of the young ones, who are to be sustained by those that got them, till they are able to shift and provide for themselves. This rule, which the infinite wise Maker hath set to the works of his hands, we find the inferior creatures steadily obey. In those viviparous ani-

mals which feed on grass, the *conjunction between male and female* lasts no longer than the very act of copulation: because the teat of the dam being sufficient to nourish the young, till it be able to feed on grass, the male only begets, but concerns not himself for the female or young, to whose sustenance he can contribute nothing. But in beasts of prey the *conjunction* lasts longer: because the dam not being able well to subsist herself and nourish her numerous offspring by her own prey alone, a more laborious, as well as more dangerous way of living than by feeding on grass, the assistance of the male is necessary to the maintenance of their common family, which cannot subsist till they are able to prey for themselves, but by the joint care of male and female. The same is observed in all birds (except some domestic ones, where plenty of food excuses the cock from feeding and taking care of the young brood) whose young needing food in the nest, the cock and hen continue mates till the young are able to use their wing, and provide for themselves.

80. And herein I think lies the chief, if not the only reason, *why the male and female in mankind are tied to a longer conjunction* than other creatures, *viz.* because the female is capable of conceiving, and *de facto* is commonly with child again, and brings forth too a new birth long before the former is out of a dependency for support on his parents' help, and able to shift for himself, and has all the assistance is due to him from his parents: whereby the father, who is bound to take care for those he hath begot, is under an obligation to continue in conjugal society with the same woman longer than other creatures, whose young being able to subsist of themselves, before the time of procreation returns again, the conjugal bond dissolves of itself, and they are at liberty, till *Hymen,*[1] at his usual anniversary season, summons them again to choose new mates. Wherein one cannot but admire the wisdom of the great Creator; who having given to man foresight and an ability to lay up for the future, as well as to supply the present necessity, hath made it necessary, that *society of man and wife should be more lasting* than of male and female amongst

[1]***Hymen:*** the god of marriage in Greek mythology.

other creatures; that so their industry might be encouraged, and their interest better united, to make provision, and lay up goods for their common issue, which uncertain mixture, or easy and frequent solutions of conjugal society would mightily disturb.

81. But though these are ties upon *mankind* which make the *conjugal bonds* more firm and lasting in man, than the other species of animals; yet it would give one reason to inquire why this *compact,* where procreation and education are secured, and inheritance taken care for, may not be made determinable, either by consent, or at a certain time, or upon certain conditions, as well as any other voluntary compacts, there being no necessity in the nature of the thing, nor to the ends of it, that it should always be for life; I mean, to such as are under no restraint of any positive law, which ordains all such contracts to be perpetual.

82. But the husband and wife, though they have but one common concern, yet having different understandings, will unavoidably sometimes have different wills too; it therefore being necessary that the last determination, i.e., the rule, should be placed somewhere; it naturally falls to the man's share, as the abler and the stronger. But this reaching but to the things of their common interest and property, leaves the wife in the full and free possession of what by contract is her peculiar right, and gives the husband no more power over her life, than she has over his. The *power of the husband* being so far from that of an absolute monarch, that the *wife* has, in many cases, a liberty to *separate* from him; where natural right, or their contract allows it, whether that contract be made by themselves in the state of nature, or by the customs or laws of the country they live in; and the children upon such separation fall to the father or mother's lot, as such contract does determine.

83. For all the ends of *marriage* being to be obtained under politic government, as well as in the state of nature, the civil magistrate doth not abridge the right, or power of either naturally necessary to those ends, *viz.* procreation and mutual support and assistance whilst they are together; but only decides any controversy that may arise between man and wife about them. If it were otherwise, and that absolute *sovereignty* and power of life and death

naturally belonged to the husband, and were *necessary to the society between man and wife,* there could be no matrimony in any of those countries where the husband is allowed no such absolute authority. But the ends of matrimony requiring no such power in the husband, the condition of *conjugal society* put it not in him, it being not at all necessary to that state. *Conjugal society* could subsist and attain its ends without it; nay, community of goods, and the power over them, mutual assistance, and maintenance, and other things belonging to *conjugal society,* might be varied and regulated by that contract, which unites man and wife in that society, as far as may consist with procreation and the bringing up of children till they could shift for themselves; nothing being necessary to any society, that is not necessary to the ends for which it is made.

84. The *society betwixt parents and children,* and the distinct rights and powers belonging respectively to them, I have treated of so largely in the foregoing chapter, that I shall not here need to say anything of it. And I think it is plain, that it is far different from a politic society.

85. *Master* and *servant* are names as old as history, but given to those of far different condition; for a free man makes himself a servant to another, by selling him for a certain time, the service he undertakes to do, in exchange for wages he is to receive: and though this commonly puts him into the family of his master, and under the ordinary discipline thereof; yet it gives the master but a temporary power over him, and no greater, than what is contained in the *contract* between 'em. But there is another sort of servants, which by a peculiar name we call *slaves,* who being captives taken in a just war, are by the right of nature subjected to the absolute dominion and arbitrary power of their masters. These men having, as I say, forfeited their lives, and with it their liberties, and lost their estates; and being in the *state of slavery,* not capable of any property, cannot in the state be considered as any part of *civil society* the chief end whereof is the preservation of property.

86. Let us therefore consider a *master of a family* with all these subordinate relations of *wife, children, servants* and *slaves* united under the domestic rule of a family; which what resemblance soever it may have in its order, offices, and number too, with a little commonwealth, yet is very far

from it, both in its constitution, power, and end: or if it must be thought a monarchy, and the *paterfamilias* the absolute monarch in it, absolute monarchy will have but a very shattered and short power, when 'tis plain by what has been said before, that the *master of the family* has a very distinct and differently limited *power*, both as to time and extent, over those several persons that are in it; for excepting the slave (and the family is as much a family, and his power as *paterfamilias* as great, whether there be any slaves[2] in his family or no) he has no legislative power of life and death over any of them, and none too but what a *mistress of a family* may have as well as he. And he certainly can have no absolute power over the whole *family*, who has but a very limited one over every individual in it. But how a *family*, or any other society of men differ from that which is properly *political society*, we shall best see by considering wherein *political society* itself consists.

87. Man being born, as has been proved, with a title to perfect freedom, and an uncontrolled enjoyment of all the rights and privileges of the law of nature, equally with any other man, or number of men in the world, hath by nature a power, not only to preserve his property, that is, his life, liberty, and estate, against the injuries and attempts of other men; but to judge of, and punish the breaches of that law in others, as he is persuaded the offence deserves, even with death itself, in crimes where the heinousness of the fact, in his opinion, requires it. But because no *political society* can be, nor subsist, without having in it self the power to preserve the property, and in order thereunto punish the offences of all those of that society; there, and there only is political society, where every one of the members hath quitted this natural power, resigned it up into the hands of the community in all cases that exclude him not from appealing for protection to the law established by it. And thus all private judgement of every particular member being excluded, the community comes to be umpire, by settled standing rules; indifferent, and the same to all parties; and

[2]**whether there by any slaves:** Cf. Aristotle, *Politics*, Book I, 1253b, 4–5: "a complete household is composed of slaves and freemen" (translated by H. Rackham).

by men having authority from the community, for the execution of those rules, decides all the differences that may happen between any members of that society, concerning any matter of right, and punishes those offences, which any member hath committed against the society with such penalties as the law has established: whereby it is easy to discern who are, and who are not, in *political society* together. Those who are united into one body, and have a common established law and judicature to appeal to, with authority to decide controversies between them, and punish offenders, *are in civil society* one with another: but those who have no such common appeal, I mean on earth, are still in the state of nature, each being, where there is no other, judge for himself and executioner; which is, as I have before showed it, the perfect *state of nature.*

88. And thus the commonwealth comes by a power to set down, what punishment shall belong to the several transgressions which they think worthy of it, committed amongst the members of that society, (which is the *power of making laws*) as well as it has the power to punish any injury done unto any of its members, by anyone that is not of it, (which is the *power of war and peace*); and all this for the preservation of property of all the members of that society, as far as is possible. But though every man who has entered into civil society, and is become a member of any commonwealth has thereby quitted his power to punish offences against the law of nature, in prosecution of his own private judgement; yet with the judgement of offences which he has given up to the legislative in all cases, where he can appeal to the magistrate, he has given up a right to the commonwealth to employ his force,[3] for the execution of the judgements of the commonwealth, whenever he shall be called to it; which indeed are his own judgements, they being made by himself, or his representative. And herein we have the original of the *legislative* and *executive power* of civil society, which is to judge by standing laws how far offences are to be

[3]**to employ his force:** Locke thus emphatically lays the basis for the legal induction of citizens into the armed forces, if that should be judged necessary by the properly elected legislative power.

punished, when committed within the commonwealth; and also to determine by occasional judgements founded on the present circumstances of the fact, how far injuries from without are to be vindicated, and in both these to employ all the force of all the members when there shall be need.

89. Wherever therefore any number of men are so united into one society, as to quit everyone his executive power of the law of nature, and to resign it to the public, there and there only is a *political,* or *civil society.* And this is done wherever any number of men, in the state of nature, enter into society to make one people, one body politic under one supreme government, or else when anyone joins himself to and incorporates with any government already made. For hereby he authorizes the society, or which is all one, the legislative thereof to make laws for him as the public good of the society shall require; to the execution whereof, his own assistance (as to his own decrees) is due. And this *puts men* out of a state of nature *into* that of a *commonwealth,* by setting up a judge on earth, with authority to determine all the controversies, and redress the injuries, that may happen to any member of the commonwealth; which judge is the legistlative, or magistrates appointed by it. And wherever there are any number of men, however associated, that have no such decisive power to appeal to, there they are still *in the state of nature.*

90. Hence it is evident, that *absolute monarchy,* which by some men is counted the only government in the world, is indeed *inconsistent with civil society,* and so can be no form of civil government at all. For the *end of civil society,* being to avoid and remedy those inconveniencies of the state of nature, which necessarily follow from every man's being judge in his own case, by setting up a known authority, to which every one of that society may appeal upon any injury received, or controversy that may arise, and which everyone of the society ought to obey;* wherever any

*'*The public power of all society is above every soul contained in the same society; and the principal use of that power is to give laws unto all that are under it, which laws in such cases we must obey, unless there be reason showed which may necessarily enforce, that the law of reason, or of God, doth enjoin the contrary.*'—Hooker's *Eccl. Pol.*, lib. i, sect. 16.

persons are who have not such an authority to appeal to, for the decision of any difference between them, there those persons are still in the *state of nature.* And so is every *absolute prince* in respect of those who are under his *dominion.*

91. For he being supposed to have all, both legislative and executive power in himself alone, there is no judge to be found, no appeal lies open to anyone, who may fairly, and indifferently, and with authority decide, and from whose decision relief and redress may be expected of any injury or inconveniency that may be suffered from the prince or by his order: So that such a man, however entitled, *Czar,* or *Grand Signior,* or how you please, is as much *in the state of nature,* with all under his dominion, as he is with the rest of mankind. For wherever any two men are, who have no standing rule, and common judge to appeal to on earth for the determination of controversies of right betwixt them, there they are still *in the state of nature,* and under all the inconveniencies of it, with only this woeful difference to the subject, or rather slave of an absolute prince:* That whereas, in the ordinary state of nature, he

*'*To take away all such mutual grievances, injuries, and wrongs,* i.e., such as attend men in the state of nature.[4] *There was no way but only by growing into composition and agreement amongst themselves, by ordaining some kind of government public, and by yielding themselves subject thereunto, that unto whom they granted authority to rule and govern, by them the peace, tranquility, and happy estate of the rest might be procured. Men always knew that where force and injury was offered, they might be defenders of themselves; they knew that, however men may seek their own commodity; yet if this were done with injury unto others, it was not to be suffered, but by all men and all good means to be withstood. Finally, they knew that no man might, in reason take upon him to determine his own right, and according to his own determination proceed in maintenance thereof, in as much as every man is towards himself, and them whom he greatly affects, partial; and therefore that strifes and troubles would be endless, except they gave their common consent, all to be ordered by some whom, they should agree upon, without which consent there would be no reason that one man should take upon him to be lord or judge over another.*—Hooker's *Eccl. Pol.*, lib. i, sect. 10.

[4]**such as attend men in the state of nature:** Locke interjects this inter-

has a liberty to judge of his right, and according to the best of his power, to maintain it; now whenever his property is invaded by the will and order of his monarch, he has not only no appeal, as those in society ought to have, but as if he were degraded from the common state of rational creatures, is denied a liberty to judge of, or to defend his right, and so is exposed to all the misery and inconveniencies that a man can fear from one, who being in the unrestrained state of nature, is yet corrupted with flattery, and armed with power.

92. For he that thinks *absolute power purifies men's bloods,* and corrects the baseness of human nature, need read but the history of this, or any other age to be convinced of the contrary. He that would have been insolent and injurious in the woods of *America,* would not probably be much better in a throne; where perhaps learning and religion shall be found out to justify, all that he shall do to his subjects, and the sword presently silence all those that dare question it. For what the *protection of absolute monarchy* is, what kind of fathers of their countries it makes princes to be, and to what a degree of happiness and security it carries civil society, where this sort of government is grown to perfection, he that will look into the late relation of *Ceylon*[5] may easily see.

93. In *absolute monarchies* indeed, as well as other governments of the world, the subjects have an appeal to the law, and judges to decide any controversies, and restrain any violence that may happen betwixt the subjects themselves, one amongst another. This everyone thinks necessary, and believes he deserves to be thought a declared enemy to society and mankind, who should go about to take it away. But whether this be from a true love of mankind and society, and such a charity as we owe all one to another, there is reason to doubt. For this is no more, than what every man, who loves his own power, profit, or greatness, may,

---

pretive comment into the quotation from Hooker, but Hooker never uses the phrase "state of nature."

[5]***Ceylon:*** Locke alludes to a travel book by Robert Knox, *An Historical Relation of the Island of Ceylon,* 1680.

and naturally must do, keep those animals from hurting or destroying one another who labour and drudge only for his pleasure and advantage, and so are taken care of, not out of any love the master has for them, but love of himself, and the profit they bring him. For if it be asked what security, *what fence* is there in such a state *against the violence and oppression of this absolute ruler?* The very question can scarce be borne. They are ready to tell you, that it deserves death only to ask after safety. Betwixt subject and subject, they will grant, there must be measures, laws, and judges for their mutual peace and security: But as for the *ruler,* he ought to be *absolute,* and is above all such circumstances: because he has a power to do more hurt and wrong, 'tis right when he does it. To ask how you may be guarded from harm, or injury on that side where the strongest hand is to do it, is presently the voice of faction and rebellion. As if when men quitting the state of nature entered into society, they agreed that all of them but one, should be under the restraint of laws, but that he should still retain all the liberty of the state of nature, increased with power, and made licentious by impunity. This is to think that men are so foolish that they take care to avoid what mischiefs may be done them by *polecats,* or *foxes,* but are content, nay think it safety, to be devoured by *lions.*

94. But whatever flatterers may talk to amuse people's understandings, it hinders not men from feeling: and when they perceive, that any man, in what station soever, is out of the bounds of the civil society which they are of; and that they have no appeal on earth against any harm they may receive from him, they are apt to think themselves in the state of nature, in respect of him, whom they find to be so; and to take care as soon as they can, to have that *safety and security in civil society,* for which it was first instituted, and for which only they entered into it. And therefore, though perhaps at first, (as shall be showed more at large hereafter, in the following part of this Discourse) some one good and excellent man, having got a pre-eminency amongst the rest, had this deference paid to his goodness and virtue, as to a kind of natural authority, that the chief rule, with arbitration of their differences, by a tacit consent devolved into his hands, without any other caution, but the assurance they had of his uprightness and wisdom: yet

when time, giving authority, and (as some men would persuade us) sacredness to customs, which the negligent and unforeseeing innocence of the first ages began, had brought in successors of another stamp, the people finding their properties not secure under the government as then it was* (whereas government has no other end but the preservation of property) could never be safe nor at rest, *nor think themselves in civil society,* till the legislative was placed in collective bodies of men, call them senate, parliament, or what you please. By which means every single person became subject, equally with other the meanest men, to those laws, which he himself, as part of the legislative had established: nor could anyone, by his own authority, avoid the force of the law, when once made, nor by any pretence of superiority, plead exemption, thereby to license his own, or the miscarriages of any of his dependents. *No man in civil society can be exempted from the laws of it.* For if any man may do, what he thinks fit, and there be no appeal on earth, for redress or security against any harm he shall do; I ask, whether he be not perfectly still in the state of nature, and so can be *no part or member of that civil society:* unless anyone will say the state of nature and civil society are one and the same thing, which I have never yet found anyone so great a patron of anarchy as to affirm†

*'*At the first, when some certain kind of regiment was once appointed, it may be that nothing was then further thought upon for the manner of governing, but all permitted unto their wisdom and discretion which were to rule, till by experience they found this for all parts very inconvenient, so as the thing which they had devised for a remedy, did indeed but increase the sore, which it should have cured. They saw, that* to live by one man's will became the cause of all men's misery. *This constrained them to come unto laws wherein all men might see their duty beforehand, and know the penalties of transgressing them.*'—Hooker's *Eccl. Pol.*, lib. i, sect. 10.

†'*Civil law being the act of the whole body politic, doth therefore overrule each several part of the same body.*'—Hooker's *Eccl. Pol.*, lib. i, sect. 10.

VIII
Of the Beginning of Political Societies

95. Men being, as has been said, by nature, all free, equal, and independent, no one can be put out of his estate, and subjected to the political power of another, without his own *consent.* The only way whereby any one divests himself of his natural liberty, and *puts on the bonds of civil society* is by agreeing with other men to join and unite into a community, for their comfortable, safe, and peaceable living one amongst another, in a secure enjoyment of their properties, and a greater security against any that are not of it. This any number of men may do, because it injures not the freedom of the rest; they are left as they were in the liberty of the state of nature. When any number of men have so *consented to make one community* or government, they are thereby presently incorporated, and make *one body politic,* wherein the *majority* have a right to act and conclude the rest.

96. For, when any number of men have, by the consent of every individual, made a *community,* they have thereby made that *community* one body, with a power to act as one body, which is only by the will and determination of the *majority.* For that which acts any community, being only the consent of the individuals of it, and it being necessary to that which is one body to move one way; it is necessary the body should move that way whither the greater force carries it, which is the *consent of the majority:* or else it is impossible it should act or continue one body, *one community,* which the consent of every individual that united into it, agreed that it should; and so everyone is bound by that consent to be concluded by the *majority.* And therefore we

see that in assemblies empowered to act by positive laws where no number is set by that positive law which empowers them, the *act of the majority* passes for the act of the whole, and of course determines as having by the law of nature and reason, the power of the whole.

97. And thus every man, by consenting with others to make one body politic under one government, puts himself under an obligation to everyone of that society, to submit to the determination of the *majority,* and to be concluded by it; or else this *original compact,* whereby he with others incorporates into *one society,* would signify nothing, and be no compact if he be left free, and under no other ties, than he was in before in the state of nature. For what appearance would there be of any compact? What new engagement if he were no farther tied by any decrees of the society, than he himself thought fit and did actually consent to? This would be still as great a liberty, as he himself had before his compact, or anyone else in the state of nature hath, who may submit himself and consent to any acts of it if he thinks fit.

98. For if the *consent of the majority* shall not in reason, be received, as *the act of the whole,* and conclude every individual; nothing but the consent of every individual can make any thing to be the act of the whole: But such a consent is next impossible ever to be had, if we consider the infirmities of health, and avocations of business, which in a number, though much less than that of a commonwealth, will necessarily keep many away from the public assembly. To which if we add the variety of opinions, and contrariety of interests, which unavoidably happen in all collections of men, the coming into society upon such terms, would be only like *Cato's*[1] coming into the theatre, only to go out again. Such a constitution as this would make the mighty *Leviathan*[2] of a shorter duration than the feeblest creatures;

[1]***Cato's:*** Locke alludes to Cato the Younger (95 B.C.–46 B.C.), a noble Roman who sought to temper the extravagance of the theatrical entertainments of a voluptuous Rome. Cf. Plutarch, *The Lives of the Noble Grecians and Romans,* "Cato the Younger."

[2]**mighty *Leviathan:*** cf. the title of Hobbes' most famous book: *Leviathan, or the Matter, Form and Power of a Commonwealth, Ecclesias-*

and not let it outlast the day it was born in: which cannot be supposed, till we can think, that rational creatures should desire and constitute societies only to be dissolved. For where the *majority* cannot conclude the rest, there they cannot act as one body, and consequently will be immediately dissolved again.

99. Whosoever therefore out of a state of nature unite into a *community*, must be understood to give up all the power, necessary to the ends for which they unite into society, to the *majority* of the community, unless they expressly agreed in any number greater than the majority. And this is done by barely agreeing to *unite into one political society*, which is *all the compact* that is, or needs be, between the individuals, that enter into, or make up a *commonwealth*. And thus, that which begins and actually *constitutes any political society*, is nothing but the consent of any number of freemen capable of a majority to unite and incorporate into such a society. And this is that, and that only, which did, or could give *beginning* to any *lawful government* in the world.

100. To this I find two objections made:

First, *That there are no instances to be found in story of a company of men independent and equal one amongst another, that met together, and in this way began and set up a government.*

Secondly, *'Tis impossible of right that men should do so, because all men being born under government, they are to submit to that, and are not at liberty to begin a new one.*

101. To the first there is this to answer. That it is not at all to be wondered, that *history* gives us but a very little account of men *that lived together in the state of nature*. The inconveniencies of that condition, and the love, and want of society no sooner brought any number of them together, but they presently united and incorporated, if they designed to continue together. And if we may not suppose *men* ever to have been *in the state of nature*, because we hear

---

tical and Civil. Locke's use of this phrase in the context of a discussion of the binding power of the "consent of the majority" suggests that he thought it crucial to underscore the submission of the individual to *duly-enacted* majority decisions. Locke thus knows nothing of an alleged individual right to "civil disobedience."

not much of them in such a state, we may as well suppose the armies of *Salmanasser* or *Xerxes*[3] were never children, because we hear little of them till they were men and embodied in armies. Government is everywhere antecedent to records, and letters seldom come in amongst a people, till a long continuation of civil society has, by other more necessary arts provided for their safety, ease, and plenty. And then they begin to look after the history of their *founders,* and search into their *original,* when they have outlived the memory of it. For 'tis with *commonwealths* as with particular persons, they are commonly *ignorant of their own births* and *infancies:* and if they know any thing of their *original,* they are beholding, for it, to the accidental records that others have kept of it. And those that we have of the beginning of any polities in the world, excepting that of the *Jews,* where God himself immediately interposed, and which favours not at all paternal dominion, are all either plain instances of such a beginning as I have mentioned, or at least have manifest footsteps of it.

102. He must show a strange inclination to deny evident matter of fact, when it agrees not with his hypothesis, who will not allow that the *beginning of Rome* and *Venice*[4] were by the uniting together of several men free and independent one of another, amongst whom there was no natural superiority or subjection. And if *Josephus Acosta's* word[5] may be taken, he tells us, that in many parts of *America* there was no government at all. *There are great and apparent*

[3]***Salmanasser* or *Xerxes:*** two ancient conquerors: the first was an Assyrian (9th century B.C.); the second a Persian (5th century B.C.).

[4]**Rome and *Venice:*** Locke's treatment here of the "founding" of ancient cities is obviously very sketchy. That sketchiness is connected to the need to emphasize the origin of legitimate government in "consent." But cf. Machiavelli's *Discourses on Livy* (Book I), a book Locke owned by at least 1678.

[5]**Acosta's word:** Joseph Acosta was a Spanish missionary. His *The Natural and Moral History of the Indies* appeared in an English translation in 1604. A close comparison of Locke and Acosta suggests that Locke has given a very partial account—to say the least—of Acosta's description of the Indians. Consider just this one remark by Acosta: the Indians "go in troupes like savage beasts" (Book VI, Chapter 19).

conjectures, says he, *that these men,* speaking of those of Peru, *for a long time had neither kings nor commonwealths, but lived in troops, as they do this day in Florida, the Cheriquanas, those of Brazil, and many other nations, which have no certain kings, but as occasion is offered in peace or war, they choose their captains as they please,* l. i. c. 25. If it be said, that every man there was born subject to his father, or the head of his family. That the subjection due from a child to a father, took not away his freedom of uniting into what political society he thought fit, has been already proved. But be that as it will, these men, 'tis evident, were actually *free;* and whatever superiority some politicians now would place in any of them, they themselves claimed it not; but by consent were all *equal,* till by the same consent they set rulers over themselves. So that their *politic societies* all began from a voluntary union, and the mutual agreement of men freely acting in the choice of their governors, and forms of government.

103. And I hope those who went away from *Sparta,* with *Palantus,* mentioned by *Justin* 1. 3. c. 4.[6] will be allowed to have been *free men independent* one of another, and to have set up a government over themselves, by their own consent. Thus I have given several examples out of history, of *people free and in the state of nature,* that being met together incorporated and *began a commonwealth.* And if the want of such instances be an argument to prove that *government* were not, nor could not be so *begun,* I suppose the contenders for paternal empire were better let it alone, than urge it against natural liberty. For if they can give so many instances out of history of *governments begun* upon paternal right, I think (though at best an argument from what has been, to what should of right be, has no great force) one might, without any great danger, yield them the

[6]***Justin:*** a Roman historian. His book, entitled *History of the World,* is based on a lost work by Trogus Pompeius. Just as Locke in the immediately preceding section gave a very partial account of Acosta's description of the Indians in Peru, so here he gives a very partial account of Justin's description of what Palantus and the other Spartans did. What they did, in fact, was to attack the citadel of the Tarentines, drive out the inhabitants, and then claim the place for their own—in short, a case of founding a new "commonwealth" by conquest.

cause. But if I might advise them in the case, they would do well not to search too much into the *original of governments* as they have begun *de facto*,[7] lest they should find at the foundation of most of them, something very little favourable to the design they promote, and such a power as they contend for.

104. But to conclude, Reason being plain on our side, that men are naturally free, and the examples of history showing that the *governments* of the world, that were begun in peace, had their beginning laid on that foundation, and were made by *the consent of the people;* there can be little room for doubt, either where the right is, or what has been the opinion, or practice of mankind, about the *first erecting of governments.*

105. I will not deny, that if we look back as far as history will direct us, towards the *original of commonwealths,* we shall generally find them under the government and administration of one man. And I am also apt to believe, that where a family was numerous enough to subsist by itself, and continued entire together, without mixing with others, as it often happens, where there is much land few people, the government commonly began in the father. For the father having, by the law of nature, the same power with every man else to punish, as he thought fit, any offences against that law, might thereby punish his transgressing children even when they were men, and out of their pupilage; and they were very likely to submit to his punishment, and all join with him against the offender, in their turns, giving him thereby power to execute his sentence against any transgression, and so in effect make him the law-maker and governor over all that remained in conjunction with his family. He was fittest to be trusted; paternal affection secured their property and interest under his care, and the custom of obeying him, in their childhood,

[7]***original of governments. . . de facto:*** Locke counsels against looking too closely into the *de facto* origin of governments. Again, cf. Machiavelli, *Discourses*, Book I. And cf. Locke, Section 121, where he refers to men as forming a new commonwealth *in vacuis locis,* or in an *empty* space, which is certainly not the case of Palantus and the other Spartans.

made it easier to submit to him rather than to any other. If therefore they must have one to rule them, as government is hardly to be avoided amongst men that live together; who so likely to be the man, as he that was their common father; unless negligence, cruelty, or any other defect of mind or body, made him unfit for it? But when either the father died, and left his next heir for want of age, wisdom, courage, or any other qualities, less fit for rule: or where several families met and consented to continue together: there, 'tis not to be doubted, but they used their natural freedom, to set up him, whom they judged the ablest and most likely, to rule well over them. Conformable hereunto we find the people of *America,* who (living out of the reach of the conquering swords and spreading domination of the two great empires of *Peru* and *Mexico*) enjoyed their own natural freedom, though, *coeteris paribus,*[8] they commonly prefer the heir of their deceased king; yet if they find him any way weak, or uncapable, they pass him by and set up the stoutest and bravest man for their ruler.

106. Thus, though looking back as far as records give us any account of peopling the world, and the history of nations, we commonly find the *government* to be in one hand, yet it destroys not that which I affirm (*viz.*) that the *beginning of politic society* depends upon the consent of the individuals to join into and make one society; who, when they are thus incorporated, might set up what form of government they thought fit. But this having given occasion to men to mistake, and think, that by nature government was monarchical, and belonged to the father, it may not be amiss here to consider, why people in the beginning generally pitched upon this form, which though perhaps the father's pre-eminency might in the first institution of some commonwealths, give a rise to, and place, in the beginning, the power in one hand; yet it is plain, that the reason that continued the form of *government in a single person,* was not any regard or respect to paternal authority; since all petty *monarchies,* that is, almost all monarchies, near their original, have been commonly, at least upon occasion, *elective.*

107. First then, in the beginning of things, the father's

[8]***coeteris paribus:*** other things being equal.

government of the childhood of those sprung from him, having accustomed them to the *rule of one man,* and taught them that where it was exercised with care and skill, with affection and love to those under it, it was sufficient to procure and preserve to men all the political happiness they sought for, in society. It was no wonder, that they should pitch upon, and naturally run into that form of government, which from their infancy they had been all accustomed to; and which, by experience, they had found both easy and safe. To which, if we add, that *monarchy* being simple, and most obvious to men, whom neither experience had instructed in forms of government, nor the ambition or insolence of empire had taught to beware of the encroachments of prerogative, or the inconveniencies of absolute power, which monarchy, in succession, was apt to lay claim to, and bring upon them, it was not at all strange, that they should not much trouble themselves to think of methods of restraining any exorbitances of those to whom they had given the authority over them, and of balancing the power of government, by placing several parts of it in different hands. They had neither felt the oppression of tyrannical dominion, nor did the fashion of the age, nor their possessions, or way of living (which afforded little matter for covetousness or ambition) give them any reason to apprehend or provide against it: and therefore 'tis no wonder they put themselves into such a *frame of government,* as was not only as I said, most obvious and simple, but also best suited to their present state and condition; which stood more in need of defence against foreign invasions and injuries, than of multiplicity of laws. The equality of a simple poor way of living confining their desires within the narrow bounds of each man's small property made few controversies and so no need of many laws to decide them: And they wanted not of justice where there were but few trespasses, and few offenders. Since then those, who liked one another so well as to join into society, cannot but be supposed to have some acquaintance and friendship together, and some trust one in another; they could not but have greater apprehensions of others than of one another: and therefore their first care and thought cannot but be supposed to be, how to secure themselves against foreign force. 'Twas natural for them to put themselves under a *frame of government,* which might best serve to that end; and choose the wisest and bravest man to conduct them in their wars, and lead them out against their enemies, and in this chiefly be their *ruler.*

108. Thus we see that the *kings* of the *Indians* in *America,* which is still a pattern of the first ages in *Asia* and *Europe,* whilst the inhabitants were too few for the country, and want of people and money gave men no temptation to enlarge their possessions of land, or contest for wider extent of ground, are little more than *generals of their armies;* and though they command absolutely in war, yet at home and in time of peace they exercise very little dominion, and have but a very moderate sovereignty, the resolutions of peace and war, being ordinarily either in the people, or in a council. Though the war itself, which admits not of plurality of governors, naturally devolves the command into the *king's sole authority.*

109. And thus in *Israel* itself, the *chief business of their judges, and first kings* seems to have been *to be captains in war* and leaders of their armies; which (besides what is signified by *going out and in before the people,*[9] which was, to march forth to war, and home again in the heads of their forces) appears plainly in the story of Jephtha. The *Ammonites* making war upon *Israel,* the *Gileadites,* in fear send to *Jephtha,* a bastard of their family, whom they had cast off, and article with him, if he will assist them against the *Ammonites,* to make him their ruler; which they do in these words: *And the people made him head and captain over them,* Judges 11.11 II, which was, as it seems, all one as to be *judge. And he judged Israel,* Judges, 12.7,, that is, was their *captain-general six years.* So when *Jotham* upbraids the *Shechemites* with the obligation they had to *Gideon,* who had been their *judge* and ruler, he tells them, *He fought for you, and adventured his life far, and delivered you out of the hands of Midian,* Judges, 9.17. Nothing mentioned of him but what

[9]***going out and in before the people:*** Locke alludes to Old Testament passages that treat the practices of leaders among the Jews. See in particular the account of Moses asking the Lord for a successor, in *Numbers* 27. Also see *Deuteronomy* 21:2; *I Samuel* 8:20; 2 *Chronicles* 1:10.

he did as a *general,* and indeed that is all is found in his history, or in any of the rest of the judges. And *Abimelech* particularly is called *king,* though at most he was but their *general.* And when, being weary of the ill-conduct of *Samuel's* sons, the children of *Israel* desired a king, *like all the nations, to judge them, and to go out before them, and to fight their battles,* 1 Sam. 8.20, God granting their desire, says to *Samuel, I will send thee a man, and thou shalt anoint him to be captain over my people Israel, that he may save my people out of the hands of the Philistines,* c. 9. v. 16. As if the only *business of a king* had been to lead out their armies, and fight in their defence; and accordingly at his inauguration, pouring a vial of oil upon him, declares to Saul, that *the Lord had anointed him to be captain over his inheritance,* c. 10. v. 1. And therefore those, who, after *Saul's* being solemnly chosen and saluted *king* by the *tribes* at *Mispah,* were unwilling to have him their king, make no other objection but this, *How shall this man save us?* v. 27, as if they should have said, This man is unfit to be our *king,* not having skill and conduct enough in war to be able to defend us. And when God resolved to transfer the government to *David,* it is in these words, *But now thy kingdom shall not continue: the Lord hath sought him a man after his own heart, and the Lord hath commanded him to be captain over his people,* c. 13. v. 14. As if the whole *kingly authority* were nothing else but to be their *general:* and therefore the *tribes* who had stuck to *Saul's* family, and opposed *David's* reign, when they came to *Hebron* with terms of submission to him, they tell him, amongst other arguments they had to submit to him as to their king, That he was in effect their *king* in *Saul's* time, and therefore they had no reason but to receive him as their *king* now. *Also* (say they) *in time past, when Saul was king over us, thou wast he that leddest out and broughtest in Israel, and the Lord said unto thee, Thou shalt feed my people Israel, and thou shalt be a captain over Israel.*[10]

110. Thus, whether *a family* by degrees *grew up into a commonwealth,* and the fatherly authority being continued on to the elder son, every one in his turn growing up under it, tacitly submitted to it, and the easiness and equality

[10]***Also . . . Israel:*** See 2 *Samuel* 5:2.

of it not offending any one, every one acquiesced, till time seemed to have confirmed it and settled a right of succession by prescription: or whether several families, or the descendants of several families, whom chance, neighbourhood, or business brought together, uniting into society, the need of a general, whose conduct might defend them against their enemies in war, and the great confidence the innocence and sincerity of that poor but virtuous age (such as are almost all those which begin *governments* that ever come to last in the world) gave men one of another, made the first beginners of commonwealths generally put the rule into one man's hand, without any other express limitation or restraint, but what the nature of the thing and the end of government required: which ever of these it was, that at first put the rule into the hands of a single person, certain it is that no body was ever entrusted with it but for the public good and safety, and to those ends in the infancies of commonwealths those who had it, commonly used it: And unless they had done so, young societies could not have subsisted: without such nursing fathers tender and carefull of the public weal, all governments would have sunk under the weakness and infirmities of their infancy; and the prince and the people had soon perished together.

111. But though the *golden age* (before vain ambition, and *amor sceleratus habendi,* evil concupiscence, had corrupted men's minds into a mistake of true power and honour) had more virtue, and consequently better governors, as well as less vicious subjects; and there was then *no stretching prerogative* on the one side to oppress the people; *nor* consequently on the other any *dispute about privilege,* to lessen or restrain the power of the magistrate; and so no contest betwixt rulers and people about governors or government:* Yet, when ambition and luxury, in future ages

*'*At first, when some certain kind of regiment was once approved, it may be nothing was then further thought upon for the manner of governing, but all permitted unto their wisdom and discretion which were to rule till by experience they found this for all parts very inconvenient, so as the thing which they had devised for a remedy did indeed but increase the sore which it should have cured. They saw that* to live by one man's will became the cause of all men's misery. *This constrained them to come unto laws wherein all men might see*

would retain and increase the power, without doing the business, for which it was given, and aided by flattery, taught princes to have distinct and separate interests from their people, men found it necessary to examine more carefully *the original* and rights of *government;* and to find out ways to *restrain the exorbitances* and *prevent the abuses* of that power which they having entrusted in another's hands only for their own good, they found was made use of to hurt them.

112. Thus we may see how probable it is that people that were naturally free, and by their own consent either submitted to the government of their father, or united together, out of different families, to make a government, should generally put the *rule into one man's hands,* and choose to be under the conduct of a *single person,* without so much as by express conditions limiting or regulating his power, which they thought safe enough in his honesty and prudence. Though they never dreamed of monarchy being *jure Divino,*[11] which we never heard of among mankind, till it was revealed to us by the divinity of this last age nor ever allowed paternal power to have a right to dominion, or to be the foundation of all government. And thus much may suffice to show, that as far as we have any light from history, we have reason to conclude, that all peaceful beginnings of *government* have been *laid in the consent of the people.* I say *peaceful,* because I shall have occasion in another place to speak of conquest, which some esteem a way of beginning of governments.

The other objection I find urged against the beginning of polities, in the way I have mentioned, is this, viz.:

113. *That all men being born under government, some or other, it is impossible any of them should ever be free, and at liberty to unite together, and begin a new one, or ever be able to erect a lawful government.*

---

their duty beforehand, and know the penatlies of transgressing them.' —Hooker's *Eccl. Pol.*, lib. i, sect. 10.

[11]***jure Divino:*** by Divine Law—cf. Filmer, *Patriarcha* and the doctrine of rulers such as James I.

If this argument be good; I ask, How came so many lawful monarchies into the world? For if anybody, upon this supposition, can show me any one man, in any age of the world, free to begin a lawful monarchy; I will be bound to show him ten other *free men* at liberty, at the same time to unite and begin a new government under a regal, or any other form. It being demonstration, that if anyone, *born under the domination* of another may be so *free* as to have a right to command others in a new and distinct empire; everyone that is *born under the dominion* of another may be so *free* too, and may become a ruler, or subject, of a distinct separate government. And so by this their own principle, either all men, however *born,* are *free,* or else there is but one lawful prince, one lawful government in the world. And then they have nothing to do but barely to show us, which that is. Which when they have done, I doubt not but all mankind will easily agree to pay obedience to him.

114. Though it be a sufficient answer to their objection to show, that it involves them in the same difficulties that it doth those they use it against; yet I shall endeavour to discover the weakness of this argument a little farther.

All men, say they, *are born under government, and therefore they cannot be at liberty to begin a new one. Everyone is born a subject to his father, or his prince, and is therefore under the perpetual tie of subjection and allegiance.* 'Tis plain mankind never owned nor considered any such natural *subjection that they were born in,* to one or to the other, that tied them, without their own consents, to a subjection to them and their heirs.

115. For there are no examples so frequent in history, both sacred and profane, as those of men withdrawing themselves, and their obedience, from the jurisdiction they were born under, and the family or community they were bred up in, and *setting up new governments* in other places; from whence sprang all that number of petty commonwealths in the beginning of ages, and which always multiplied, as long as there was room enough, till the stronger, or more fortunate swallowed the weaker; and those great ones again breaking to pieces, dissolved into lesser dominions. All which are so many testimonies against paternal sovereignty, and plainly prove, that it was not the natural right of the father descending to his heirs that made gov-

ernments in the beginning, since it was impossible, upon that ground, there should have been so many little kingdoms; all must have been but only one universal monarchy if men had not been *at liberty to separate* themselves from their families, and the government, be it what it will, that was set up in it, and go and make distinct commonwealths and other governments, as they thought fit.

116. This has been the practice of the world from its first beginning to this day: nor is it now any more hindrance to the freedom of mankind, that they are *born under constituted and ancient polities,* that have established laws and set forms of government, than if they were born in the woods, amongst the unconfined inhabitants that ran loose in them. For those who would persuade us, that *by being born under any government, we are naturally subjects to it,* and have no more any title or pretence to the freedom of the state of nature, have no other reason (bating that of paternal power, which we have already answered) to produce for it, but only because our fathers or progenitors passed away their natural liberty, and thereby bound up themselves and their posterity to a perpetual subjection to the government which they themselves submitted to. 'Tis true, that whatever engagements or promises anyone has made for himself, he is under the obligation of them, but *cannot* by any *compact* whatsoever, bind *his children* or posterity. For his son, when a man, being altogether as free as the father, any *act of the father can no more give away the liberty of the son,* than it can of anybody else: He may indeed annex such conditions to the land, he enjoyed as a subject of any commonwealth, as may oblige his son to be of that community, if he will enjoy those possessions which were his father's; because that estate being his father's property, he may dispose or settle it as he pleases.

117. And this has generally given the occasion to mistake in this matter; because commonwealths not permitting any part of their dominions to be dismembered, nor to be enjoyed by any but those of their community, the son cannot ordinarily enjoy the possessions of his father but under the same terms his father did; by becoming a member of the society: whereby he puts himself presently under the government, he finds there established, as much as any other subject of that commonwealth. And thus *the consent of*

free-men, born under government, which only *makes them members of it,* being given separately in their turns, as each comes to be of age, and not in a multitude together; people take no notice of it, and thinking it not done at all, or not necessary, conclude they are naturally subjects as they are men.

118. But 'tis plain *governments* themselves understand it otherwise; they *claim no power over the son, because of that they had over the father;* nor look on children as being their subjects, by their fathers being so. If a subject of *England* have a child by an *English* woman in *France,* whose subject is he? Not the King of *England's;* for he must have leave to be admitted to the privileges of it. Nor the King of *France's;* for how then has his father a liberty to bring him away, and breed him as he pleases? And whoever was judged as a *traitor* or *deserter,* if he left, or warred against a country, for being barely born in it of parents that were aliens there? 'Tis plain then, by the practice of governments themselves, as well as by the law of right reason, that a *child is born a subject of no country or government.* He is under his father's tuition and authority till he come to age of discretion; and then he is a freeman, at liberty what government he will put himself under; what body politic he will unite himself to. For if an *English-man's* son, born in *France,* be at liberty, and may do so, it is evident there is no tie upon him by his father's being a subject of this kingdom; nor is he bound up, by any compact of his ancestors. And why then hath not his son, by the same reason, the same liberty, though he be born anywhere else? Since the power that a father hath naturally over his children, is the same, wherever they be born; and the ties of natural obligations are not bounded by the positive limits of kingdoms and common-wealths.

119. *Every man* being, as has been showed, *naturally free,* and nothing being able to put him into subjection to any earthly power, but only his own consent; it is to be considered what shall be understood to be a *sufficient declaration of* a man's *consent, to make him subject* to the laws of any government. There is a common distinction of an express and a tacit consent, which will concern our present case. No body doubts but an *express consent* of any man, entering into any society, makes him a perfect member of that soci-

ety, a subject of that government. The difficulty is, what ought to be looked upon as a *tacit consent,* and how far it binds, *i.e.,* how far anyone shall be looked on to have consented, and thereby submitted to any government, where he has made no expressions of it at all. And to this I say, that every man that hath any possession, or enjoyment, of any part of the dominions of any government, doth thereby give his *tacit consent,* and is as far forth obliged to obedience to the laws of that government, during such enjoyment, as any one under it; whether this his possession be of land, to him and his heirs for ever, or a lodging only for a week; or whether it be barely travelling freely on the highway; and in effect, it reaches as far as the very being of anyone within the territories of that government.

120. To understand this the better, it is fit to consider, that every man when he at first incorporates himself into any commonwealth, he, by his uniting himself thereunto, annexes also, and submits to the community those possessions, which he has, or shall acquire, that do not already belong to any other government. For it would be a direct contradiction, for anyone, to enter into society with others for the securing and regulating of property: and yet to suppose his land, whose property is to be regulated by the laws of the society, should be exempt from the jurisdiction of that government to which he himself the proprietor of the land, is a subject. By the same act therefore, whereby anyone unites his person, which was before free, to any commonwealth; by the same he unites his possessions, which were before free, to it also; and they become, both of them, person and possession, subject to the government and dominion of that commonwealth, as long as it hath a being. *Whoever* therefore, from thenceforth, by inheritance, purchase, permission, or otherwise *enjoys any part of the land* so annexed to, and under the government *of that commonwealth, must take it with the condition* it is under; that is, *of submitting to the government of the commonwealth,* under whose jurisdiction it is, as far forth, as any subject of it.

121. But since the government has a direct jurisdiction only over the land and reaches the possessor of it (before he has actually incorporated himself in the society) only as he dwells upon and enjoys that; *the obligation* anyone is under, by virtue of such enjoyment, *to submit to the government*

begins and ends with the enjoyment; so that whenever the owner, who has given nothing but such a *tacit consent* to the government, will, by donation, sale, or otherwise, quit the said possession, he is at liberty to go and incorporate himself into any other commonwealth, or to agree with others to begin a new one, *in vacuis locis,*[12] in any part of the world, they can find free and unpossessed: whereas he, that has once, by actual agreement, and any *express* declaration, given his *consent* to be of any commonweal, is perpetually and indispensably obliged to be and remain unalterably a subject to it, and can never be again in the liberty of the state of nature; unless by any calamity, the government he was under comes to be dissoved; or else by some public act cuts him off from being any longer a member of it.

122. But submitting to the laws of any country, living quietly, and enjoying privileges and protection under them, *makes not a man a member of that society;* this is only a local protection and homage due to, and from all those who, not being in a state of war, come within the territories belonging to any government, to all parts whereof the force of its law extends. But this no more *makes a man a member of that society,* a perpetual subject of that commonwealth, than it would make a man a subject to another in whose family he found it convenient to abide for some time; though, whilst he continued in it, he were obliged to comply with the laws and submit to the government he found there. And thus we see that *foreigners,* by living all their lives under another government, and enjoying the privileges and protection of it, though they are bound, even in conscience, to submit to its administration, as far forth as any denizen; yet do not thereby come to be *subjects or members of that commonwealth.* Nothing can make any man so, but his actually entering into it by positive engagement, and express promise and compact. This is that, which I think, concerning the beginning of political societies, and that *consent which makes anyone a member* of any commonwealth.

[12]***in vacuis locis:*** in an empty space. Cf. Locke's use of Justin, above, in Section 103.

IX

Of the Ends of Political Society and Government

123. If man in the state of nature be so free, as has been said; if he be absolute lord of his own person and possessions, equal to the greatest, and subject to no body, why will he part with his freedom? Why will he give up this empire, and subject himself to the dominion and control of any other power? To which 'tis obvious to answer, that though in the state of nature he hath such a right, yet the enjoyment of it is very uncertain and constantly exposed to the invasion of others. For all being kings as much as he, every man is equal, and the greater part no strict observers of equity and justice, the enjoyment of the property he has in this state is very unsafe, very unsecure. This makes him willing to quit a condition, which however free, is full of fears and continual dangers: and 'tis not without reason, that he seeks out, and is willing to join in society with others who are already united, or have a mind to unite for the mutual *preservation* of their lives, liberties, and estates, which I call by the general name, *property.*

124. The great and *chief end* therefore, of men's uniting into commonwealths, and putting themselves under government, *is the preservation of their property.* To which in the state of nature there are many things wanting.

First, There wants an *established,* settled, known *law,* received and allowed by common consent to be the standard of right and wrong, and the common measure to decide all controversies between them. For though the law of nature be plain and intelligible to all rational creatures; yet men being biased by their interest, as well as ignorant for want of study of it, are not apt to allow of it as a law binding to them in the application of it to their particular cases.

125. *Secondly,* In the state of nature there wants *a known and indifferent judge,* with authority to determine all differences according to the established law. For everyone in that state being both judge and executioner of the law of nature, men being partial to themselves, passion and revenge is very apt to carry them too far, and with too much heat in their own cases; as well as negligence and unconcernedness, to make them too remiss in other men's.

126. *Thirdly,* In the state of nature there often wants *power* to back and support the sentence when right, and to *give* it due *execution.* They who by any injustice offended, will seldom fail, where they are able, by force to make good their injustice: such resistance many times makes the punishment dangerous, and frequently destructive, to those who attempt it.

127. Thus mankind, notwithstanding all the privileges of the state of nature, being but in an ill condition, while they remain in it, are quickly driven into society. Hence it comes to pass, that we seldom find any number of men live any time together in this state. The inconveniencies, that they are therein exposed to, by the irregular and uncertain exercise of the power every man has of punishing the transgressions of others, make them take sanctuary under the established laws of government, and therein seek *the preservation of their property.* 'Tis this makes them so willingly give up every one his single power of punishing to be exercised by such alone as shall be appointed to it amongst them; and by such rules as the community, or those authorized by them to that purpose, shall agree on. And in this we have the original *right and rise* of both *the legislative and executive power* as well as of the governments and societies themselves.

128. For in the state of nature, to omit the liberty he has of innocent delights, a man has two powers.

The first is to do whatsoever he thinks fit for the preservation of himself and others within the permission of the *law of nature:* by which law common to them all, he and all the rest of *mankind are one community,* make up one society distinct from all other creatures. And were it not for the corruption, and viciousness of degenerate men, there would be no need of any other; no necessity that men should separate from this great and natural community, and by positive agreements combine into smaller and divided associations.

The other power a man has in the state of nature, is the *power to punish the crimes* committed against that law. Both these he gives up when he joins in a private, if I may so call it, or particular political society, and incorporates into any commonwealth, separate from the rest of mankind.

129. The first *power, viz. of doing whatsoever he thought fit for the preservation of himself,* and the rest of mankind, *he gives up* to be regulated by laws made by the society, so far forth as the preservation of himself, and the rest of that society shall require; which laws of the society in many things confine the liberty he had by the law of nature.

130. *Secondly,* The *power of punishing* he wholly *gives up,* and engages his natural force (which he might before employ in the execution of the law of nature, by his own single authority, as he thought fit) to assist the executive power of the society as the law thereof shall require. For being now in a new state, wherein he is to enjoy many conveniencies from the labour, assistance, and society of others in the same community, as well as protection from its whole strength; he is to part also with as much of his natural liberty in providing for himself, as the good, prosperity, and safety of the society shall require: which is not only necessary but just; since the other members of the society do the like.

131. But though men when they enter into society, give up the equality, liberty, and executive power they had in the state of nature, into the hands of the society, to be so far disposed of by the legislative, as the good of the society shall require; yet it being only with an intention in every-one the better to preserve himself his liberty and property; (for no rational creature can be supposed to change his condition with an intention to be worse), the power of the society, or *legislative* constituted by them, *can never be supposed to extend farther than the common good;* but is obliged to secure every one's property by providing against those three defects above-mentioned, that made the state of nature so unsafe and uneasy. And so whoever has the legislative or supreme power of any commonwealth, is bound to

govern by established *standing laws,* promulgated and known to the people, and not by extemporary decrees; by *indifferent* and upright *judges,* who are to decide controversies by those laws; and to employ the force of the community at home, *only in the execution of such laws,* or abroad to prevent or redress foreign injuries, and secure the community from inroads and invasion. And all this to be directed to no other *end,* but the *peace, safety,* and *public good* of the people.

X
Of the Forms of a Commonwealth

132. The majority having, as has been showed, upon men's first uniting into society, the whole power of the community, naturally in them, may employ all that power in making laws for the community from time to time, and executing those laws by officers of their own appointing; and then the *form* of the government is a perfect *democracy:* or else may put the power of making laws into the hands of a few select *men,* and their heirs or successors; and then it is an *oligarchy:* or else into the hands of one man, and then it is a *monarchy:* if to him and his heirs, it is a *hereditary monarchy:* if to him only for life, but upon his death the power only of nominating a successor to return to them; an *elective monarchy.* And so accordingly of these the community may make compounded and mixed forms of government, as they think good. And if the legislative power be at first given by the majority to one or more persons only for their lives, or any limited time, and then the supreme power to revert to them again; when it is so reverted, the community may dispose of it again anew into what hands they please, and so constitute a new form of government; for the *form of government depending upon the placing* the supreme power, which is the *legislative,* it being impossible to conceive that an inferior power should prescribe to a superior, or any but the supreme make laws, according as the power of making laws is placed, such is *the form of the commonwealth.*

133. By *commonwealth,* I must be understood all along to mean, not a democracy, or any form of government, but *any independent community* which the *Latins* signified by the

word *civitas,* to which the word which best answers in our language, is *Common-wealth,* and most properly expresses such a society of men which Community or City in *English* does not, for there may be subordinate communities in a government; and City amongst us has a quite different notion from Commonwealth: And therefore to avoid ambiguity, I crave leave to use the word *commonwealth* in that sense, in which I find it used by King *James the First,* and I take it to be its genuine signification; which if any body dislike, I consent with him to change it for a better.

XI

Of the Extent of the Legislative Power

134. The great end of men's entering into society, being the enjoyment of their properties in peace and safety, and the great instrument and means of that being the laws established in that society; the *first and fundamental positive law* of all commonwealths *is the establishing of the legislative power;* as the *first and fundamental natural law,* which is to govern even the legislative itself, is *the preservation of the society,* and (as far as will consist with the public good) of every person in it. This *legislative* is not only the *supreme power* of the commonwealth, but sacred and unalterable in the hands where the community have once placed it; nor can any edict of anybody else, in what form soever conceived, or by what power soever backed, have the force and obligation of a *law,* which has not its *sanction from* that *legislative* which the public has chosen and appointed. For without this the law could not have that, which is absolutely necessary to its being a *law, the consent of the society,* over whom nobody can have a power to make laws* but by their

*'*The lawful power of making laws to command whole politic societies of men belonging so properly unto the same entire societies, that for any prince or potentate of what kind soever upon earth, to exercise the same of himself, and not by express commission immediately and personally received from God, or else by authority derived at the first from their consent, upon whose persons they impose laws, it is no better than mere tyranny. Laws they are not therefore, which public approbation hath not made so.*'—Hooker's *Eccl. Pol.*, lib. i, sect. 10. '*Of this point therefore we are to note that such men naturally have no full and perfect power to command whole politic multitudes of*

own consent, and by authority received from them; and therefore all the *obedience,* which by the most solemn ties anyone can be obliged to pay, ultimately terminates in this *supreme power,* and is directed by those laws which it enacts: Nor can any oaths to any foreign power whatsoever, or any domestic subordinate power, discharge any member of the society from his *obedience to the legislative,* acting pursuant to their trust, nor oblige him to any obedience contrary to the laws so enacted, or farther than they do allow; it being ridiculous to imagine one can be tied ultimately to *obey* any *power* in the society, which is not *the supreme.*

135. Though the *legislative,* whether placed in one or more, whether it be always in being, or only by intervals, though it be the supreme power in every commonwealth; yet,

First, It is *not,* nor can possibly be absolutely *arbitrary* over the lives and fortunes of the people. For it being but the joint power of every member of the society given up to that person, or assembly, which is legislator, it can be no more than those persons had in a state of nature before they entered into society, and gave up to the community. For no body can transfer to another more power than he has in himself; and no body has an absolute arbitrary power over himself, or over any other, to destroy his own life, or take away the life or property of another. A man, as has been proved, cannot subject himself to the arbitrary power of another; and having in the state of nature no arbitrary power over the life, liberty, or possession of another, but only so much as the law of nature gave him for the preservation of himself, and the rest of mankind; this is all he doth, or can give up to the commonwealth, and by it to the *legislative power,* so that the legislative can have no more than this. Their power in the utmost bounds of it, *is limited*

---

men, therefore utterly without our consent we could in such sort be at no man's commandment living. And to be commanded, we do consent when that society, whereof we be a part, hath at any time before consented, without revoking the same after by the like universal agreement.

'Laws therefore human, of what kind soever, are available by consent.'—Hooker's *Eccl. Pol.*, Ibid.

to the public good of the society.* It is a power that hath no other end but preservation, and therefore can never have a right to destroy, enslave, or designedly to impoverish the subjects. The obligations of the law of nature, cease not in society, but only in many cases are drawn closer, and have by human laws known penalties annexed to them to enforce their observation. Thus the law of nature stands as an eternal rule to all men, *legislators* as well as others. The *rules* that they make for other men's actions, must, as well as their own and other men's actions, be conformable to the law of nature, *i.e.* to the will of God, of which that is a declaration, and the *fundamental law of nature* being *the preservation of mankind,* no human sanction can be good, or valid against it.

136. *Secondly,* The *legislative* or supreme authority cannot assume to itself a power to rule by extemporary arbitrary decrees, but *is bound to dispense justice* and decide the rights of the subject *by promulgated standing laws,*† *and known*

*'*Two foundations there are which bear up public societies, the one a natural inclination whereby all men desire sociable life and fellowship; the other an order, expressly or secretly agreed upon, touching the manner of their union in living together; the latter is that which we call the law of a commonweal, the very soul of a politic body, the parts whereof are by law animated, held together, and set on work in such actions as the common good requireth. Laws politic, ordained for external order and regiment amongst men, are never framed as they should be, unless presuming the will of man to be inwardly obstinate, rebellious, and averse from all obedience to the sacred laws of his nature; in a word, unless presuming man to be in regard of his depraved mind, little better than a wild beast, they do accordingly provide notwithstanding, so to frame his outward actions, that they be no hindrance unto the common good, for which societies are instituted. Unless they do this they are not perfect.*'—Hooker's *Eccl. Pol.*, lib. i, sect 10.

†'*Human laws are measures in respect of men, whose actions they must direct, howbeit such measures they are as have also their higher rules to be measured by, which rules are two, the law of God and the law of Nature; so that laws human must be made according to the general laws of Nature, and without contradiction to any positive law of Scripture, otherwise they are ill made.*'—Hooker's *Eccl. Pol.*, lib. iii, sect. 9.

'*To constrain men to anything inconvenient doth seem unreasonable.*'—Ibid., lib. i, sect. 10.

authorized judges. For the law of nature being unwritten, and so nowhere to be found but in the minds of men, they who through passion or interest shall miscite, or misapply it, cannot so easily be convinced of their mistake where there is no established judge: and so it serves not, as it ought, to determine the rights, and fence the properties of those that live under it, especially where everyone is judge, interpreter, and executioner of it too, and that in his own case: and he that has right on his side, having ordinarily but his own single strength, hath not force enough to defend himself from injuries or to punish delinquents. To avoid these inconveniencies which disorder men's properties in the state of nature, men unite into societies, that they may have the united strength of the whole society to secure and defend their properties, and may have *standing rules* to bound it, by which everyone may know what is his. To this end it is that men give up all their natural power to the society which they enter into, and the community put the legislative power into such hands as they think fit, with this trust, that they shall be governed by *declared laws,* or else their peace, quiet, and property will still be at the same uncertainty, as it was in the state of nature.

137. Absolute arbitrary power, or governing without *settled standing laws,* can neither of them consist with the ends of society and government, which men would not quit the freedom of the state of nature for, and tie themselves up under, were it not to preserve their lives, liberties, and fortunes; and by *stated rules* of right and property to secure their peace and quiet. It cannot be supposed that they should intend, had they a power so to do, to give to any one, or more, an *absolute arbitrary power* over their persons and estates, and put a force into the magistrate's hand to execute his unlimited will arbitrarily upon them: this were to put themselves into a worse condition than the state of nature, wherein they had a liberty to defend their right against the injuries of others, and were upon equal terms of force to maintain it, whether invaded by a single man, or many in combination. Whereas by supposing they have given up themselves to the *absolute arbitrary power* and will of a legislator, they have disarmed themselves, and armed him, to make a prey of them when he pleases. He being in a much worse condition who is exposed to the arbitrary

power of one man who has the command of a hundred thousand than he that is exposed to the arbitrary power of a hundred thousand single men: no body being secure, that his will who has such a command, is better than that of other men, though his force be a hundred thousand times stronger. And therefore whatever form the commonwealth is under, the ruling power ought to govern by *declared* and *received laws,* and not by extemporary dictates and undetermined resolutions, for then mankind will be in a far worse condition, than in the state of nature, if they shall have armed one or a few men with the joint power of a multitude, to force them to obey at pleasure the exorbitant and unlimited decrees of their sudden thoughts, or unrestrained, and till that moment unknown wills without having any measures set down which may guide and justify their actions. For all the power the government has, being only for the good of the society, as it ought not to be *arbitrary* and at pleasure, so it ought to be exercised by *established and promulgated laws:* that both the people may know their duty, and be safe and secure within the limits of the law, and the rulers too kept within their due bounds, and not to be tempted by the power they have in their hands, to employ it to such purposes, and by such measures, as they would not have known, and own not willingly.

138. *Thirdly,* The *supreme power cannot take* from any man any part of his *property* without his own consent. For the preservation of property being the end of government, and that for which men enter into society, it necessarily supposes and requires, that the people should *have property,* without which they must be supposed to lose that by entering into society, which was the end for which they entered into it, too gross an absurdity for any man to own. *Men* therefore *in society having property,* they have such a right to the goods, which by the law of the community are theirs, that no body hath a right to take their substance, or any part of it from them, without their own consent; without this, they have no property at all. For I have truly no *property* in that which another can by right take from me, when he pleases, against my consent. Hence it is a mistake to think, that the supreme or *legislative* power of any commonwealth, can do what it will, and dispose of the estates of the subject *arbitrarily,* or take any part of them at plea-

sure. This is not much to be feared in governments where the *legislative* consists, wholly or in part, in assemblies which are variable, whose members upon the dissolution of the assembly, are subjects under the common laws of their country, equally with the rest. But in governments, where the *legislative* is in one lasting assembly always in being, or in one man as in absolute monarchies, there is danger still, that they will think themselves to have a distinct interest from the rest of the community; and so will be apt to increase their own riches and power, by taking, what they think fit, from the people. For a man's *property* is not at all secure, though there be good and equitable laws to set the bounds of it between him and his fellow-subjects, if he who commands those subjects, have power to take from any private man what part he pleases of his *property,* and use and dispose of it as he thinks good.

139. But *government* into whatsoever hands it is put, being as I have before showed, entrusted with this condition, and *for this end,* that men might have and secure *their properties,* the prince or senate, however it may have power to make laws for the regulating of *property* between the subjects one amongst another, yet can never have a power to take to themselves the whole or any part of the subjects' *property,* without their own consent. For this would be in effect to leave them no *property* at all. And to let us see, that *even absolute power,* where it is necessary, is *not arbitrary* by being absolute, but is still limited by that reason, and confined to those ends, which required it in some cases to be absolute, we need look no farther than the common practice of martial discipline. For the preservation of the army, and in it of the whole commonwealth, requires an *absolute obedience* to the command of every superior officer, and it is justly death to disobey or dispute the most dangerous or unreasonable of them: but yet we see, that neither the sergeant, that could command a soldier to march up to the mouth of a cannon, or stand in a breach, where he is almost sure to perish, can command that soldier to give him one penny of his money; nor the *general* that can condemn him to death for deserting his post, or for not obeying the most desperate orders, can yet with all his absolute power of life and death, dispose of one farthing of that soldier's estate, or seize one jot of his goods; whom yet he can com-

mand anything, and hang for the least disobedience. Because such a blind obedience is necessary to that end for which the commander has his power, *viz.* the preservation of the rest; but the disposing of his goods has nothing to do with it.

140. 'Tis true, governments cannot be supported without great charge, and 'tis fit everyone who enjoys his share of the protection, should pay out of his estate his proportion for the maintenance of it. But still it must be with his own consent, *i.e.* the consent of the majority, giving it either by themselves, or their representatives chosen by them. For if anyone shall claim a *power to lay* and levy *taxes* on the people, by his own authority, and without such consent of the people, he thereby invades the *fundamental law of property,* and subverts the end of government. For what property have I in that which another may by right take, when he pleases to himself?

141. *Fourthly,* The *legislative cannot transfer the power of making laws* to any other hands, for it being but a delegated power from the people, they who have it, cannot pass it over to others. The people alone can appoint the form of the commonwealth, which is by constituting the legislative, and appointing in whose hands that shall be. And when the people have said, We will submit to rules, and be governed by *laws* made by such men, and in such forms, no body else can say other men shall make *laws* for them; nor can the people be bound by any *laws* but such as are enacted by those, whom they have chosen, and authorized to make *laws* for them. The power of the *legislative* being derived from the people by a positive voluntary grant and institution, can be no other, than what that positive grant conveyed, which being only to make *laws,* and not to make *legislators,* the *legislative* can have no power to transfer their authority of making laws, and place it in other hands.

142. These are the *bounds* which the trust that is put in them by the society, and the law of God and nature, have *set to the legislative* power of every commonwealth, in all forms of government.

First, They are to govern by *promulgated established laws,* not to be varied in particular cases, but to have one rule for rich and poor, for the favourite at court, and the country man at plough.

Secondly, These *laws* also ought to be designed *for* no other end ultimately but *the good of the people.*

Thirdly, They must *not raise taxes* on the property of the people, *without the consent of the people,* given by themselves or their deputies. And this properly concerns only such governments where the *legislative* is always in being, or at least where the people have not reserved any part of the legislative to deputies, to be from time to time chosen by themselves.

Fourthly, The *legislative* neither must *nor can transfer the power of making laws* to anybody else, or place it anywhere but where the people have.

XII
Of the Legislative, Executive, and Federative Power of the Commonwealth

143. The *legislative* power is that which has a right *to direct* how *the force of the commonwealth* shall be employed for preserving the community and the members of it. But because those laws which are constantly to be executed, and whose force is always to continue, may be made in a little time; therefore there is no need, that the *legislative* should be always in being, not having always business to do. And because it may be too great temptation to human frailty apt to grasp at power, for the same persons who have the power of making laws, to have also in their hands the power to execute them, whereby they may exempt themselves from obedience to the laws they make, and suit the law, both in its making and execution, to their own private advantage, and thereby come to have a distinct interest from the rest of the community, contrary to the end of society and government: Therefore in well-ordered commonwealths, where the good of the whole is so considered, as it ought, the *legislative* power is put into the hands of divers persons who duly assembled, have by themselves, or jointly with others, a power to make laws, which when they have done, being separated again, they are themselves subject to the laws they have made; which is a new and near tie upon them, to take care, that they make them for the public good.

144. But because the laws, that are at once, and in a short time made, have a constant and lasting force, and need a *perpetual execution,* or an attendance thereunto:

therefore 'tis necessary there should be a *power always in being,* which should see to the *execution* of the laws that are made, and remain in force. And thus the *legislative* and *executive power*[1] come often to be separated.

145. There is another *power* in every commonwealth which one may call *natural,* because it is that which answers to the power every man naturally had before he entered into society. For though in a commonwealth the members of it are distinct persons still in reference to one another, and as such are governed by the laws of the society; yet in reference to the rest of mankind, they make one body, which is, as every member of it before was, still in the state of nature with the rest of mankind. Hence it is, that the controversies that happen between any man of the society with those that are out of it, are managed by the public; and an injury done to a member of their body, engages the whole in the reparation of it. So that under this consideration the whole community is one body in the state of nature, in respect of all other states or persons out of its community.

146. This therefore contains the power of war and peace, leagues and alliances, and all the transactions, with all persons and communities without the commonwealth, and may be called *federative,* if any one pleases. So the thing be understood, I am indifferent as to the name.

147. These two powers, *executive* and *federative,* though they be really distinct in themselves, yet one comprehending the *execution* of the municipal laws of the society *within* its self, upon all that are parts of it; the other the management of the *security and interest of the public without,* with all those that it may receive benefit or damage from, yet they are always almost united. And though this *federative power* in the well or ill management of it be of great moment to the commonwealth, yet it is much less capable to be directed by antecedent, standing, positive laws than the *executive;* and so must necessarily be left to the prudence and wis-

[1]**execution** . . . ***executive power:*** Locke does not explicitly separate off the judicial aspect of the "executive" power, but it is clear that in his doctrine of government to execute includes *to judge* as well as *to enforce*.

dom of those whose hands it is in, to be managed for the public good. For the *laws* that concern subjects one amongst another, being to direct their actions, may well enough *precede* them. But what is to be done in reference to *foreigners,* depending much upon their actions, and the variation of designs and interests, must be *left* in great part *to* the *prudence* of those who have this power committed to them, to be managed by the best of their skill, for the advantage of the commonwealth.

148. Though, as I said, the *executive* and *federative power* of every community be really distinct in themselves, yet they are hardly to be separated, and placed, at the same time, in the hands of distinct persons. For both of them requiring the force of the society for their exercise, it is almost impracticable to place the force of the commonwealth in distinct, and not subordinate hands; or that the *executive* and *federative power* should be *placed* in persons that might act separately, whereby the force of the public would be under different commands: which would be apt sometime or other to cause disorder and ruin.

XIII
Of the Subordination of the Powers of the Commonwealth

149. Though in a constituted commonwealth standing upon its own basis, and acting according to its own nature, that is, acting for the preservation of the community, there can be but *one supreme power,* which is *the legislative,* to which all the rest are and must be subordinate, yet the legislative being only a fiduciary power to act for certain ends, there remains still *in the people a supreme power* to remove or *alter the legislative,* when they find the *legislative* act contrary to the trust reposed in them. For all *power given with trust* for the attaining an *end,* being limited by that end, whenever that end is manifestly neglected, or opposed, the *trust* must necessarily be *forfeited,* and the power devolve into the hands of those that gave it, who may place it anew where they shall think best for their safety and security. And thus the *community* perpetually *retains a supreme power* of saving themselves from the attempts and designs of any body, even of their legislators, whenever they shall be so foolish, or so wicked, as to lay and carry on designs against the liberties and properties of the subject. For no man, or society of men, having a power to deliver up their *preservation,* or consequently the means of it, to the absolute will and arbitrary dominion of another; whenever any one shall go about to bring them into such a slavish condition, they will always have a right to preserve what they have not a power to part with; and to rid themselves of those who invade this fundamental, sacred, and unalterable law of *self-preservation,* for which they entered into society. And thus the *community* may be said in this respect to be *always the supreme power,* but not as considered under any form of govern-

ment, because this power of the people can never take place till the government be dissolved.

150. In all cases, whilst the government subsists, the *legislative is the supreme power.* For what can give laws to another, must needs be superior to him: and since the legislative is no otherwise legislative of the society, but by the right it has to make laws for all the parts, and for every member of the society, prescribing rules to their actions, and giving power of execution, where they are transgressed, the *legislative* must needs be the *supreme*, and all other powers in any members or parts of the society, derived from and subordinate to it.

151. In some commonwealths where the *legislative* is not always in being, and the *executive* is vested in a single person, who has also a share in the legislative; there that single person in a very tolerable sense may also be called *supreme;* not that he has in himself all the supreme power, which is that of law-making: but because he has in him the *supreme execution* from whom all inferior magistrates derive all their several subordinate powers, or at least the greatest part of them: having also no legislative superior to him, there being no law to be made without his consent, which cannot be expected should ever subject him to the other part of the legislative, *he is* properly enough in this sense *supreme.* But yet it is to be observed, that though *oaths of allegiance* and fealty are taken to him, 'tis not to him as *supreme legislator,* but as supreme executor of the law made, by a joint power of him with others; *allegiance* being nothing but an *obedience according to law,* which when he violates, he has no right to obedience, nor can claim it otherwise than as the public person vested with the power of the law, and so is to be considered as the image, phantom, or representative of the commonwealth, acted by the will of the society, declared in its laws; and thus he has no will, no power, but that of the law. But when he quits this representation, this public will, and acts by his own private will, he degrades himself, and is but a single private person without power, and without will, that has any right to *obedience;* the members owing no *obedience* but to the public will of the society.

152. The *executive power* placed any where but in a person, that has also a share in the legislative, is visibly subordinate and accountable to it, and may be at pleasure

changed and displaced; so that it is not the *supreme executive power* that is exempt from *subordination,* but the *supreme executive power* vested in one, who having a share in the legislative, has no distinct superior legislative to be subordinate and accountable to, farther than he himself shall join and consent: so that he is no more subordinate than he himself shall think fit, which one may certainly conclude will be but very little. Of other *ministerial* and *subordinate powers* in a commonwealth, we need not speak, they being so multiplied with infinite variety, in the different customs and constitutions of distinct commonwealths, that it is impossible to give a particular account of them all. Only thus much, which is necessary to our present purpose, we may take notice of concerning them, that they have no manner of authority any of them, beyond what is, by positive grant, and commission, delegated to them, and are all of them accountable to some other power in the commonwealth.

153. It is not necessary, no nor so much as convenient, that the *legislative* should be *always in being.* But absolutely necessary that the *executive power* should, because there is not always need of new laws to be made, but always need of execution of the laws that are made. When the *legislative* hath put the *execution* of the laws, they make, into other hands, they have a power still to resume it out of those hands, when they find cause, and to punish for any maladministration against the laws. The same holds also in regard of the *federative* power, that and the executive being both *ministerial and subordinate to the legislative,* which as has been showed in a constituted commonwealth, is the supreme. The *legislative* also in this case being supposed to consist of several persons; (for if it be a single person, it cannot but be always in being, and so will as supreme, naturally have the supreme executive power, together with the legislative), may *assemble and exercise their legislature,* at the times that either their original constitution, or their own adjournment appoints, or when they please; if neither of these hath appointed any time, or there be no other way prescribed to convoke them. For the supreme power being placed in them by the people 'tis always in them, and they may exercise it when they please, unless by their original constitution they are limited to certain seasons, or by an act of their supreme power they have adjourned to a certain

time, and when that time comes, they have a right to *assemble* and *act* again.

154. If the *legislative,* or any part of it, be made up of representatives chosen for that time by the people, which afterwards return into the ordinary state of subjects, and have no share in the legislature but upon a new choice, this power of choosing must also be exercised by the people, either at certain appointed seasons, or else when they are summoned to it: and in this latter case, the power of convoking the legislative, is ordinarily placed in the executive, and has one of these two limitations in respect of time: that either the original constitution requires their *assembling* and *acting* at certain intervals, and then the executive power does nothing but ministerially issue directions for their electing and assembling according to due forms: or else it is left to his prudence to call them by new elections, when the occasions or exigencies of the public require the amendment of old, or making of new laws, or the redress or prevention of any inconveniencies, that lie on, or threaten the people.

155. It may be demanded here, what if the executive power, being possessed of the force of the commonwealth, shall make use of that force to hinder the *meeting* and *acting of the legislative,* when the original constitution, or the public exigencies require it? I say using force upon the people without authority, and contrary to the trust put in him, that does so, is a state of war with the people, who have a right to *reinstate* their *legislative in the exercise* of their power. For having erected a legislative, with an intent they should exercise the power of making laws, either at certain set times, or when there is need of it; when they are hindered by any force from what is so necessary to the society, and wherein the safety and preservation of the people consists, the people have a right to remove it by force. In all states and conditions the true remedy of *force* without authority, is to oppose *force* to it. The use of *force* without authority, always puts him that uses it into a *state of war,* as the aggressor, and renders him liable to be treated accordingly.

156. The power of *assembling and dismissing the legislative,* placed in the executive, gives not the executive a superiority over it, but is a fiduciary trust, placed in him, for the safety of the people, in a case where the uncertainty, and

variableness of human affairs could not bear a steady fixed rule. For it not being possible, that the first framers of the government should, by any foresight, be so much masters of future events, as to be able to prefix so just periods of return and duration to the *assemblies of the legislative,* in all times to come, that might exactly answer all the exigencies of the commonwealth; the best remedy could be found for this defect, was to trust this to the prudence of one who was always to be present, and whose business it was to watch over the public good. Constant *frequent meetings of the legislative,* and long continuations of their assemblies, without necessary occasion, could not but be burthensome to the people, and must necessarily in time produce more dangerous inconveniencies, and yet the quick turn of affairs might be sometimes such as to need their present help: any delay of their *convening* might endanger the public; and sometimes too their business might be so great, that the limited time of their sitting might be too short for their work, and rob the public of that benefit, which could be had only from their mature deliberation. What then could be done, in this case, to prevent the community, from being exposed sometime or other to eminent hazard, on one side, or the other, by fixed intervals and periods, set to the *meeting and acting of the legislative,* but to entrust it to the prudence of some, who being present, and acquainted with the state of public affairs, might make use of this prerogative for the public good? And where else could this be so well placed as in his hands, who was entrusted with the execution of the laws for the same end? Thus supposing the regulation of times for the *assembling and sitting of the legislative,* not settled by the original constitution, it naturally fell into the hands of the executive, not as an arbitrary power depending on his good pleasure, but with this trust always to have it exercised only for the public weal, as the occurrences of times and change of affairs might require. Whether *settled periods of their convening,* or a *liberty* left to the prince *for convoking the legislative,* or perhaps a mixture of both, hath the least inconvenience attending it, 'tis not my business here to inquire, but only to show that, though the executive power may have the prerogative of *convoking* and *dissolving* such *conventions of the legislative,* yet it is not thereby superior to it.

157. Things of this world are in so constant a flux, that nothing remains long in the same state. Thus people, riches, trade, power, change their stations, flourishing mighty cities come to ruin, and prove in time neglected desolate corners, whilst other unfrequented places grow into populous countries filled with wealth and inhabitants. But things not always changing equally, and private interest often keeping up customs and privileges, when the reasons of them are ceased, it often comes to pass, that in governments where part of the legislative consists of *representatives* chosen by the people, that in tract of time this *representation* becomes very *unequal* and disproportionate to the reasons it was at first established upon. To what gross absurdities the following of custom, when reason has left it, may lead, we may be satisfied when we see the bare name of a town, of which there remains not so much as the ruins, where scarce so much housing as a sheep-cote or more inhabitants than a shepherd, is to be found, sends *as many representatives* to the grand assembly of law-makers, as a whole county numerous in people, and powerful in riches. This strangers stand amazed at, and every one must confess needs a remedy. Though most think it hard to find one, because the constitution of the legislative being the original and supreme act of the society, antecedent to all positive laws in it, and depending wholly on the people, no inferior power can alter it. And therefore the *people,* when the *legislative* is once constituted, *having* in such a government as we have been speaking of, *no power* to act as long as the government stands; this inconvenience is thought incapable of a remedy.

158. *Salus populi suprema lex,*[1] is certainly so just and fundamental a rule, that he, who sincerely follows it, cannot dangerously err. If therefore the executive, who has the power of convoking the legislative, observing rather the true proportion, than fashion of *representation,* regulates, not by old custom, but true reason, the *number of members,* in all places, that have a right to be distinctly represented, which no part of the people however in-

[1]***Salus . . . lex:*** the people's safety is the supreme law. Locke derives this maxim from the fundamental right to preserve oneself.

corporated can pretend to, but in proportion to the assistance, which it affords to the public, it cannot be judged to have set up a new legislative, but to have restored the old and true one, and to have rectified the disorders, which succession of time had insensibly, as well as inevitably introduced. For it being the interest, as well as intention of the people, to have a fair and *equal representative;* whoever brings it nearest to that, is an undoubted friend to, and establisher of the government, and cannot miss the consent and approbation of the community. *Prerogative* being nothing but a power in the hands of the prince to provide for the public good, in such cases, which depending upon unforeseen and uncertain occurrences, certain and unalterable laws could not safely direct, whatsoever shall be done manifestly for the good of the people, and the establishing the government upon its true foundations, is, and always will be just *prerogative.* The power of erecting new corporations, and therewith *new representatives,* carries with it a supposition, that in time the *measures of representation* might vary, and those places have a just right to be represented which before had none; and by the same reason, those cease to have a right, and be too inconsiderable for such a privilege, which before had it. 'Tis not a change from the present state, which perhaps corruption, or decay has introduced, that makes an inroad upon the government, but the tendency of it to injure or oppress the people, and to set up one part, or party, with a distinction from, and an unequal subjection of the rest. Whatsoever cannot but be acknowledged to be of advantage to the society, and people in general, upon just and lasting measures, will always, when done, justify it self; and whenever the people shall choose their *representatives upon* just and undeniably *equal measures* suitable to the original frame of the government, it cannot be doubted to be the will and act of the society, whoever permitted, or caused them so to do.

XIV
Of Prerogative

159. Where the legislative and executive power are in distinct hands, (as they are in all moderated monarchies) and well-framed governments, there the good of the society requires, that several things should be left to the discretion of him, that has the executive power. For the legislators not being able to foresee, and provide, by laws, for all that may be useful to the community, the executor of the laws, having the power in his hands, has by the common law of nature, a right to make use of it, for the good of the society, in many cases, where the municipal law has given no direction, till the legislative can conveniently be assembled to provide for it. Many things there are, which the law can by no means provide for, and those must necessarily be left to the discretion of him, that has the executive power in his hands, to be ordered by him, as the public good and advantage shall require: nay, 'tis fit that the laws themselves should in some cases give way to the executive power, or rather to this fundamental law of nature and government, *viz.*, that as much as may be, *all* the members of the society are to be *preserved*. For since many accidents may happen, wherein a strict and rigid observation of the laws may do harm; (as not to pull down an innocent man's house to stop the fire when the next to it is burning) and a man may come sometimes within the reach of the law, which makes no distinction of persons, by an action, that may deserve reward and pardon; 'tis fit, the ruler should have a power, in many cases, to mitigate the severity of the law, and pardon some offenders: For the *end of government* being the *preservation of all,* as much as may be, even the guilty are to be spared, where it can prove no prejudice to the innocent.

160. This power to act according to discretion, for the public good, without the prescription of the law, and some-

times even against it, *is* that which is called *prerogative.* For since in some governments the law-making power is not always in being, and is usually too numerous, and so too slow, for the dispatch requisite to execution: and because also it is impossible to foresee, and so by laws to provide for, all accidents and necessities, that may concern the public; or make such laws, as will do no harm, if they are executed with an inflexible rigour, on all occasions, and upon all persons, that may come in their way, therefore there is a latitude left to the executive power, to do many things of choice, which the laws do not prescribe.

161. This power whilst employed for the benefit of the community, and suitably to the trust and ends of the government, *is undoubted prerogative,* and never is questioned. For the people are very seldom, or never scrupulous, or nice in the point; they are far from examining *prerogative,* whilst it is in any tolerable degree employed for the use it was meant; that is, for the good of the people, and not manifestly against it. But if there comes to be a *question* between the executive power and the people, *about* a thing claimed as a *prerogative;* the tendency of the exercise of such *prerogative* to the good or hurt of the people, will easily decide that question.

162. It is easy to conceive, that in the infancy of governments, when commonwealths differed little from families in number of people, they differed from them too but little in number of laws: and the governors, being as the fathers of them, watching over them for their good, the government was almost all *prerogative.* A few established laws served the turn, and the discretion and care of the ruler supplied the rest. But when mistake, or flattery prevailed with weak princes to make use of this power, for private ends of their own, and not for the public good, the people were fain by express laws to get prerogative determined, in those points, wherein they found disadvantage from it: And thus declared *limitations of prerogative* were by the people found necessary in cases which they and their ancestors had left, in the utmost latitude, to the wisdom of those princes, who made no other but a right use of it, that is, for the good of their people.

163. And therefore they have a very wrong notion of government, who say, that the people have *encroached upon*

the prerogative, when they have got any part of it to be defined by positive laws. For in so doing, they have not pulled from the prince any thing, that of right belonged to him, but only declared, that that power which they indefinitely left in his or his ancestors' hands, to be exercised for their good, was not a thing, which they intended him, when he used it otherwise. For the end of government being the good of the community, whatsoever alterations are made in it, tending to that end, cannot be an *encroachment* upon any body: since no body in government can have a right tending to any other end. And those only are *encroachments* which prejudice or hinder the public good. Those who say otherwise, speak as if the prince had a distinct and separate interest from the good of the community, and was not made for it, the root and source, from which spring almost all those evils, and disorders, which happen in kingly governments. And indeed if that be so, the people under his government are not a society of rational creatures entered into a community for their mutual good; they are not such as have set rulers over themselves, to guard, and promote that good; but are to be looked on as an herd of inferior creatures, under the dominion of a master, who keeps them, and works them for his own pleasure or profit. If men were so void of reason, and brutish, as to enter into society upon such terms, *prerogative* might indeed be, what some men would have it, an arbitrary power to do things hurtful to the people.

164. But since a rational creature cannot be supposed when free, to put himself into subjection to another, for his own harm: (though where he finds a good and a wise ruler he may not perhaps think it either necessary, or useful to set precise bounds to his power in all things) *prerogative* can be nothing, but the people's permitting their rulers, to do several things of their own free choice, where the law was silent, and sometimes too against the direct letter of the law, for the public good; and their acquiescing in it when so done. For as a good prince, who is mindful of the trust put into his hands, and careful of the good of his people, cannot have too much *prerogative,* that is, power to do good: so a weak and ill prince, who would claim that power, which his predecessors exercised without the direction of the law, as a prerogative belonging to him by right

of his office, which he may exercise at his pleasure, to make or promote an interest distinct from that of the public, gives the people an occasion, to claim their right, and limit that power, which, whilst it was exercised for their good, they were content should be tacitly allowed.

165. And therefore he, that will look into the *History of England,* will find, that prerogative was always *largest* in the hands of our wisest and best princes: because the people observing the whole tendency of their actions to be the public good, contested not what was done without law to that end; or if any human frailty or mistake (for princes are but men, made as others) appeared in some small declinations from that end; yet 'twas visible the main of their conduct tended to nothing but the care of the public. The people therefore finding reason to be satisfied with these princes, whenever they acted without or contrary to the letter of the law, acquiesced in what they did, and, without the least complaint, let them enlarge their *prerogative* as they pleased, judging rightly, that they did nothing herein to the prejudice of their laws, since they acted conformable to the foundation and end of all laws, the public good.

166. Such God-like princes indeed had some title to arbitrary power, by the argument that would prove absolute monarchy the best government, as that which God Himself governs the universe by: because such kings partake of His wisdom and goodness. Upon this is founded that saying, That the reigns of good princes have been always most dangerous to the liberties of their people. For when their successors, managing the government with different thoughts, would draw the actions of those good rulers into precedent, and make them the standard of their *prerogative,* as if what had been done only for the good of the people, was a right in them to do, for the harm of the people, if they so pleased; it has often occasioned contest, and sometimes public disorders, before the people could recover their original right, and get that to be declared not to be *prerogative,* which truly was never so, since it is impossible that any body in the society should ever have a right to do the people harm; though it be very possible, and reasonable, that the people should not go about to set any bounds to the *prerogative* of those kings or rulers, who themselves transgressed not the bounds of the public good.

For *prerogative is nothing but the power of doing public good without a rule.*

167. The power of *calling Parliaments* in *England,* as to precise time, place, and duration, is certainly a *prerogative* of the king, but still with this trust, that it shall be made use of for the good of the nation, as the exigencies of the times, and variety of occasions shall require. For it being impossible to foresee, which should always be the fittest place for them to assemble in, and what the best season; the choice of these was left with the executive power, as might be most subservient to the public good, and best suit the ends of Parliaments.

168. The old question will be asked in this matter of *prerogative,* But *who shall be judge* when this power is made a right use of? I answer: Between an executive power in being, with such a prerogative, and a legislative that depends upon his will for their convening, there can be no *judge on earth:* As there can be none between the legislative, and the people, should either the executive or the legislative, when they have got the power in their hands, design, or go about to enslave, or destroy them. The people have no other remedy in this, as in all other cases where they have no judge on earth, but to *appeal to Heaven.*[1] For the rulers, in such attempts, exercising a power the people never put into their hands (who can never be supposed to consent, that any body should rule over them for their harm) do that, which they have not a right to do. And where the body of the people, or any single man, is deprived of their right, or is under the exercise of a power without right, have no appeal on earth, there they have a liberty to appeal to Heaven whenever they judge the cause of sufficient moment. And therefore, though the *people* cannot be *judge,* so as to have by the constitution of that society, any superior power, to determine and give effective sentence in the case; yet they have, by a law antecedent and paramount to all positive laws of men, reserved that ultimate determination to themselves, which belongs to all mankind, where there lies no appeal on earth, *viz.* to judge whether they have just cause to make

[1]***appeal to Heaven:*** Cf. Sections 21, 176, 241, and 242.

their appeal to heaven. And this judgment they cannot part with, it being out of a man's power so to submit himself to another, as to give him a liberty to destroy him; God and nature never allowing a man so to abandon himself, as to neglect his own preservation: And since he cannot take away his own life, neither can he give another power to take it. Nor let any one think, this lays a perpetual foundation for disorder: for this operates not till the inconvenience is so great, that the majority feel it, and weary of it, and find a necessity to have it amended. But this the executive power, or wise princes, never need come in the danger of: And 'tis the thing of all others, they have most need to avoid, as of all others the most perilous.

XV

Of Paternal, Political and Despotical Power, Considered Together

169. Though I have had occasion to speak of these separately before, yet the great mistakes of late about government, having, as I suppose, arisen from confounding these distinct powers one with another, it may not, perhaps, be amiss, to consider them here together.

170. *First* then, *paternal* or *parental power* is nothing but that, which parents have over their children, to govern them for the children's good, till they come to the use of reason, or a state of knowledge, wherein they may be supposed capable to understand that rule, whether it be the law of nature, or the municipal law of their country, they are to govern themselves by: capable, I say, to know it, as well as several others, who live, as freemen, under the law. The affection and tenderness which God hath planted in the breasts of parents, towards their children, makes it evident, that this is not intended to be a severe arbitrary government, but only for the help, instruction, and preservation of their offspring. But happen as it will, there is, as I have proved, no reason, why it should be thought to extend to life and death, at any time, over their children, more than over any body else, neither can there be any pretense why this parental power should keep the child, when grown to a man, in subjection to the will of his parents, any farther, than the having received life and education from his parents, obliges him to respect, honour, gratitude, assistance, and support all his life to both father and mother. And thus, 'tis true, the *paternal* is a natural

government, but not at all extending it self to the ends and jurisdictions of that which is political. The *power of the father doth not reach* at all to the *property* of the child, which is only in his own disposing.

171. *Secondly, political power* is that power which every man, having in the state of nature, has given up into the hands of the society, and therein to the governors, whom the society hath set over it self, with this express or tacit trust, that it shall be employed for their good, and the preservation of their property: Now this *power,* which every man has *in the state of nature,* and which he parts with to the society, in all such cases, where the society can secure him, is, to use such means for the preserving of his own property, as he thinks good, and nature allows him; and to punish the breach of the law of nature in others so, as (according to the best of his reason) may most conduce to the preservation of himself, and the rest of mankind. So that the *end and measure of this power,* when in every man's hands in the state of nature, being the preservation of all of his society, that is, all mankind in general, it can have no other *end or measure,* when in the hands of the magistrate, but to preserve the members of that society in their lives, liberties, and possessions; and so cannot be an absolute, arbitrary power over their lives and fortunes, which are as much as possible to be preserved; but a *power to make laws,* and annex such *penalties* to them, as may tend to the preservation of the whole, by cutting off those parts, and those only, which are so corrupt, that they threaten the sound and healthy, without which no severity is lawful. And this *power has its original only from compact* and agreement, and the mutual consent of those who make up the community.

172. *Thirdly, despotical power* is an absolute, arbitrary power one man has over another, to take away his life, whenever he pleases. This is a power, which neither nature gives, for it has made no such distinction between one man and another; nor compact can convey. For man not having such an arbitrary power over his own life, cannot give another man such a power over it; but it is *the effect only of forfeiture,* which the aggressor makes of his own life, when he puts himself into the state of war with another. For having quitted reason, which God hath given to be the rule betwixt man and man, and the common bond whereby hu-

man kind is united into one fellowship and society; and having renounced the way of peace, which that teaches, and made use of the force of war to compass his unjust ends upon another, where he has no right, and so revolting from his own kind to that of beasts by making force which is theirs, to be his rule of right, he renders himself liable to be destroyed by the injured person and the rest of mankind, that will join with him in the execution of justice, as any other wild beast, or noxious brute with whom mankind can have neither society nor security.[1] And thus *captives,* taken in a just and lawful war, and such only, are *subject to a despotical* power, which as it arises not from compact, so neither is it capable of any, but is the state of war continued. For what compact can be made with a man that is not master of his own life? What condition can he perform? And if he be once allowed to be master of his own life, the *despotical, arbitrary power* of his master ceases. He that is master of himself, and his own life, has a right too to the means of preserving it; so that *as soon as compact enters, slavery ceases,* and he so far quits his absolute power and puts an end to the state of war, who enters into conditions with his captive.

173. *Nature gives* the first of these *viz., paternal power to parents* for the benefit of their children during their minority, to supply their want of ability, and understanding how to manage their property. (By *property* I must be understood here, as in other places, to mean that property which men have in their persons as well as goods.) *Voluntary agreement gives* the second, *viz., political power to governors,* for the benefit of their subjects, to secure them in the possession and use of their properties. And *forfeiture* gives the third, *despotical power* to lords for their own benefit, over those who are stripped of all property.

174. He that shall consider the distinct rise and extent, and the different ends of these several powers, will plainly see, that paternal power comes as far short of that of the *magistrate,* as *despotical* exceeds it; and that *absolute dominion,* however placed, is so far from being one kind of civil soci-

[1]**with . . . security:** Locke may have meant this to read: "that is destructive to their being."

ety, that it is as inconsistent with it, as slavery is with property. *Paternal power* is only where minority makes the child incapable to manage his property; *political* where men have property in their own disposal; and *despotical* over such as have no property at all.

XVI
Of Conquest

175. Though governments can originally have no other rise than that before mentioned, nor polities be founded on any thing but *the consent of the people;* yet such has been the disorders ambition has filled the world with, that in the noise of war, which makes so great a part of the history of mankind, this *consent* is little taken notice of; and therefore many have mistaken the force of arms for the consent of the people; and reckon conquest as one of the originals of government. But *conquest* is as far from setting up any government, as demolishing a house is from building a new one in the place. Indeed it often makes way for a new frame of a commonwealth, by destroying the former; but, without the consent of the people, can never erect a new one.

176. That the *aggressor,* who puts himself into the state of war with another, and *unjustly invades* another man's right, *can,* by such an unjust war, *never* come to *have a right over the conquered,* will be easily agreed by all men, who will not think, that robbers and pirates have a right of empire over whomsoever they have force enough to master; or that men are bound by promises, which unlawful force extorts from them. Should a robber break into my house, and with a dagger at my throat, make me seal deeds to convey my estate to him, would this give him any title? Just such a title by his sword, has an *unjust conqueror,* who forces me into submission. The injury and the crime is equal, whether committed by the wearer of a crown, or some petty villain. The title of the offender, and the number of his followers make no difference in the offence, unless it be to aggravate it. The only difference is, great robbers punish little ones, to keep them in their obedience, but the great ones are rewarded with laurels and triumphs, because they

are too big for the weak hands of justice in this world, and have the power in their own possession, which should punish offenders. What is my remedy against a robber, that so broke into my house? *Appeal* to the law for justice. But perhaps justice is denied, or I am crippled and cannot stir, robbed and have not the means to do it. If God has taken away all means of seeking remedy, there is nothing left but patience. But my son, when able, may seek the relief of the law, which I am denied: he or his son may renew his *appeal* till he recover his right. But the conquered, or their children, have to court, no arbitrator on earth to appeal to. Then they may *appeal, as Jephtha* did *to Heaven,* and repeat their *appeal,* till they have recovered the native right of their ancestors, which was to have such a legislative over them, as the majority should approve, and freely acquiesce in. If it be objected, this would cause endless trouble; I answer, no more than justice does, where she lies open to all that appeal to her. He that troubles his neighbour without a cause, is punished for it by the justice of the court he appeals to. And he that *appeals to Heaven* must be sure he has right on his side; and a right too that is worth the trouble and cost of the appeal, as he will answer at a tribunal, that cannot be deceived, and will be sure to retribute to every one according to the mischiefs be hath created to his fellow-subjects; that is, any part of mankind. From whence 'tis plain, that he that *conquers in an unjust war, can* thereby *have no title to the subjection and obedience of the conquered.*

177. But supposing victory favours the right side, let us consider a *conqueror in a lawful war,* and see what power he gets, and over whom.

First, 'tis plain he *gets no power* by his conquest *over those that conquered with him.* They that fought on his side cannot suffer by the conquest, but must at least be as much free men as they were before. And most commonly they serve upon terms, and on condition to share with their leader, and enjoy a part of the spoil, and other advantages that attend the conquering sword: or at least have a part of the subdued country bestowed upon them. And *the conquering people are not,* I hope, to be *slaves by conquest,* and wear their laurels only to show they are sacrifices to their leader's triumph. They that found absolute monarchy upon the title of the sword, make their heroes, who are the founders of such monarchies, arrant *Draw-can-Sirs,*[1] and forget they had any officers and soldiers that fought on their side in the battles they won, or assisted them in the subduing, or shared in possessing the countrips they mastered. We are told by some that the *English* monarchy is founded in the *Norman* Conquest, and that our princes have thereby a title to absolute dominion: which if it were true (as by the history it appears otherwise) and that *William* had a right to make war on this island; yet his dominion by conquest could reach no farther, than to the *Saxons* and *Britons* that were then inhabitants of this country. The *Normans* that came with him, and helped to conquer, and all descended from them are freemen and no subjects by conquest; let that give what dominion it will. And if I, or any body else shall claim freedom, as derived from them, it will be very hard to prove the contrary: and 'tis plain, the law that has made no distinction between the one and the other, intends not there should be any difference in their freedom or privileges.

178. But supposing, which seldom happens, that the conquerors and conquered never incorporate into one people, under the same laws and freedom. Let us see next *what power a lawful conqueror has over the subdued;* and that I say is purely despotical. He has an abolute power over the lives of those, who by an unjust war have forfeited them; but not over the lives or fortunes of those, who engaged not in the war, nor over the possessions even of those, who were actually engaged in it.

179. *Secondly,* I say then the *conqueror* gets no power but only over those, who have actually assisted, concurred, or consented to that unjust force, that is used against him. For the people having given to their governors no power to do an unjust thing, such as is to make an unjust war, (for they never had such a power in themselves): they ought not to

[1]***Draw-can-Sirs:*** The *Oxford English Dictionary* traces this name to a blustering character in the Second Duke of Buckingham's satirical play, *The Rehearsal* (1671). In the last scene, Draw-can-Sir kills all the combatants on both sides; another character says of him that he "does what he will, without regard to manners, justice, or numbers."

be charged, as guilty of the violence and injustice that is committed in an unjust war, any farther, than they actually abet it; no more, than they are to be thought guilty of any violence or oppression their governors should use upon the people themselves, or any part of their fellow-subjects, they having empowered them no more to the one than to the other. Conquerors, 'tis true, seldom trouble themselves to make the distinction, but they willingly permit the confusion of war to sweep all together; but yet this alters not the right: for the conqueror's power over the lives of the conquered, being only because they have used force to do, or maintain an injustice, he can have that power only over those, who have concurred in that force, all the rest are innocent; and he has no more title over the people of that country, who have done him no injury, and so have made no forfeiture of their lives, than he has over any other, who, without any injuries or provocations, have lived upon fair terms with him.

180. *Thirdly,* the *power a conqueror gets* over those he overcomes *in a just war, is perfectly despotical:* he has an absolute power over the lives of those, who by putting themselves in a state of war, have forfeited them; but he has not thereby a right and title to their possessions. This I doubt not, but at first sight will seem a strange doctrine, it being so quite contrary to the practice of the world; there being nothing more familiar in speaking of the dominion of countries, than to say such an one conquered it. As if conquest, without any more ado, conveyed a right of possession. But when we consider, that the practice of the strong and powerful, how universal soever it may be, is seldom the rule of right, however it be one part of the subjection of the conquered, not to argue against the conditions, cut out to them by the conquering sword.

181. Though in all war there be usually a complication of force and damage, and the aggressor seldom fails to harm the estate, when he uses force against the persons of those he makes war upon; yet 'tis the use of force only, that puts a man into the state of war. For whether by force he begins the injury, or else having quietly, and by fraud, done the injury, he refuses to make reparation, and by force maintains it, (which is the same thing as at first to have done it by force) 'tis the unjust use of force that

makes the war. For he that breaks open my house and violently turns me out of doors; or having peaceably got in, by force keeps me out, does in effect the same thing; supposing we are in such a state, that we have no common judge on earth, whom I may appeal to, and to whom we are both obliged to submit: for of such I am now speaking. 'Tis the *unjust use of force* then, that *puts a man into the state of war* with another, and thereby he, that is guilty of it, makes a forfeiture of his life. For quitting reason, which is the rule given between man and man, and using force the way of beasts, he becomes liable to be destroyed by him he uses force against, as any savage ravenous beast, that is dangerous to his being.

182. But because the miscarriages of the father are no faults of the children, and they may be rational and peaceable, notwithstanding the brutishness and injustice of the father; the father, by his miscarriages and violence, can forfeit but his own life, and involves not his children in his guilt or destruction. His goods, which nature, that willeth the preservation of all mankind as much as is possible, hath made to belong to the children to keep them from perishing, do still continue to belong to his children. For supposing them not to have joined in the war, either through infancy, absence, or choice, they have done nothing to forefeit them: *not has the conqueror any right* to take them away, by the bare title of having subdued him, that by force attempted his destruction; though perhaps he may have some right to them, to repair the damages he has sustained by the war, and the defence of his own right, which how far it reaches to the possessions of the conquered, we shall see by and by. So that he that *by conquest has a right over a man's person* to destroy him if he pleases, has *not* thereby a right *over his estate* to possess and enjoy it. For it is the brutal force the aggressor has used, that gives his adversary a right to take away his life, and destroy him if he pleases, as a noxious creature; but 'tis damage sustained that alone gives him title to another man's goods: for though I may kill a thief that sets on me in the highway, yet I may not (which seems less) take away his money and let him go; this would be robbery on my side. His force, and the state of war he put himself in, made him forfeit his life, but gave me no title to his goods. The *right*

then *of conquest extends only to the lives* of those who joined in the war, *not to their estates,* but only in order to make reparation for the damages received, and the charges of the war, and that too with reservation of the right of the innocent wife and children.

183. Let the *conqueror* have as much justice on his side, as could be supposed, he *has* no *right* to seize more than the vanquished could forfeit; his life is at the victor's mercy, and his service and goods he may appropriate to make himself reparation; but he cannot take the goods of his wife and children; they too had a title to the goods he enjoyed, and their shares in the estate he possessed. For example, I in the state of nature (and all commonwealths are in the state of nature one with another) have injured another man, and refusing to give satisfaction, it comes to a state of war, wherein my defending by force, what I had gotten unjustly, makes me the aggressor. I am conquered: my life, 'tis true, as forfeit, is at mercy, but not my wife's and children's. They made not the war, nor assisted in it. I could not forfeit their lives, they were not mine to forfeit. My wife had a share in my estate, that neither could I forfeit. And my children also, being born of me, had a right to be maintained out of my labour or substance. Here then is the case; The conqueror has a title to reparation for damages received, and the children have a title to their father's estate for their subsistence. For as to the wife's share, whether her own labour or compact gave her a title to it, 'tis plain, her husband could not forfeit what was hers. What must be done in the case? I answer; The fundamental law of nature being, that all, as much as may be, should be preserved, it follows, that if there be not enough fully to *satisfy* both, *viz.,* for the *conqueror's losses,* and children's maintenance, he that hath, and to spare, must remit something of his full satisfaction, and give way to the pressing and preferable title of those, who are in danger to perish without it.

184. But supposing the *charge* and *damages of the war* are to be made up to the conqueror to the utmost farthing, and that the children of the vanquished, spoiled of all their father's goods, are to be left to starve and perish: yet the satisfying of what shall on this score, be due to the conqueror, will scarce give him a *title to any country he shall*

conquer. For the damages of war can scarce amount to the value of any considerable *tract of land* in any part of the world, where all the land is possessed, and none lies waste. And if I have not taken away the conqueror's land, which, being vanquished, it is impossible I should; scarce any other spoil I have done him, can amount to the value of mine, supposing it equally cultivated and of an extent any way coming near, what I had over run of his. The destruction of a year's product or two, (for it seldom reaches four or five) is the utmost spoil, that usually can be done. For as to money; and such riches and treasure taken away, these are none of nature's goods, they have but a phantastical imaginary value: nature has put no such upon them: They are of no more account by her standard, than the Wampompeke of the *Americans* to an *European* prince, or the silver money of *Europe* would have been formerly to an *American.* And five year's product is not worth the perpetual inheritance of *land,* where all is possessed, and none remains waste, to be taken up by him that is disseised[2]: which will be easily granted, if one do but take away the imaginary value of money, the disproportion being more, than between five and five hundred. Though, at the same time, half a year's product is more worth than the inheritance, where there being more *land,* than the inhabitants possess, and make use of, any one has liberty to make use of the waste: But there conquerors take little care to possess themselves of the *lands of the vanquished.* No damage therefore, that men in the state of nature (as all princes and governments are in reference to one another) suffer from one another, can give a conqueror power, to dispossess the posterity of the vanquished, and turn them out of that inheritance, which ought to be the possession of them and their descendants to all generations. The conqueror indeed will be apt to think himself master: And 'tis the very condition of the subdued not to be able to dispute their right. But if that be all, it gives no other title than what bare force gives to the stronger over the weaker. And, by this reason, he that is strongest will have a right to whatever he pleases to seize on.

[2]**disseised:** an archaic word meaning dispossessed.

185. Over those then, that joined with him in the war, and over those of the subdued country that opposed him not, and the posterity even of those that did, the conqueror, even in a just war, hath, *by* his *conquest, no right of dominion:* They are free from any subjection to him, and if their former government be dissolved, they are at liberty to begin and erect another to themselves.

186. The conqueror, 'tis true, usually, by the force he has over them, compels them, with a sword at their breasts, to stoop to his conditions, and submit to such a government as he pleases to afford them; but the inquiry is, What right he has to do so? If it be said they submit by their own consent; then this allows their own *consent* to be *necessary to give the conqueror a title to rule* over them. It remains only to be considered, whether *promies, extorted by force,* without right, can be thought consent, and *how far they bind.* To which I shall say, they *bind not at all;* because whatsoever another gets from me by force, I still retain the right of, and he is obliged presently to restore. He that forces my horse from me, ought presently to restore him, and I have still a right to retake him. By the same reason, he that *forced a promise* from me, ought presently to restore it, *i.e.,* quit me of the obligation of it; or I may resume it myself, *i.e.,* choose whether I will perform it. For the law of nature laying an obligation on me, only by the rules she prescribes, cannot oblige me by the violation of her rules: such is the extorting any thing from me by force. Nor does it at all alter the case, to say I *gave my promise,* no more than it excuses the force, and passes the right, when I put my hand in my pocket, and deliver my purse my self to a thief, who demands it with a pistol at my breast.

187. From all which it follows, that the *government of a conqueror,* imposed, by force, on the subdued, against whom he had no right of war, or who joined not in the war against him, where he had right, *has no obligation* upon them.

188. But let us suppose that all the men of that community being all members of the same body politic, may be taken to have joined in that unjust war, wherein they are subdued, and so their lives are at the mercy of the conqueror.

189. I say, this concerns not their children, who are in

their minority. For since a father hath not, in himself, a power over the life or liberty of his child; no act of his can possibly forfeit it: so that the children, whatever may have happened to the fathers, are freemen, and the absolute power of the *conqueror* reaches no farther than the persons of the men, that were subdued by him, and dies with them; and should he govern them as slaves, subjected to his absolute, arbitrary power, he *has no* such *right of dominion over their children.* He can have no power over them, but by their own consent, whatever he may drive them to say or do; and he has no lawful authority, whilst force, and not choice, compels them to submission.

190. Every man is born with a double right: *First, A right of freedom to his person,* which no other man has a power over, but the free disposal of it lies in himself. *Secondly, A right,* before any other man, to *inherit,* with his brethren, his father's goods.

191. By the first of these, a man is *naturally free* from subjection to any government, though he be born in a place under its jurisdiction. But if he disclaim the lawful government of the country he was born in, he must also quit the right that belonged to him by the laws of it, and the possessions there descending to him from his ancestors, if it wpre a government made by their consent.

192. By the second, the *inhabitants* of any country, who are descended, and derive a title to their estates from those, who are subdued, and had a government forced upon them against their free consents, *retain a right to the possession of their ancestors,* though they consent not freely to the government, whose hard conditions were by force imposed on the possessors of that country. For the first *conqueror never* having *had a title to the land* of that country, the people who are the descendants of, or claim under those, who were forced to submit to the yoke of a government by constraint, have always a right to shake it off, and free themselves from the usurpation, or tyranny which the sword hath brought in upon them, till their rulers put them under such a frame of government, as they willingly and of choice consent to. Who doubts but the Grecian Christians' descendants of the ancient possessors of that country may justly cast off the Turkish yoke which they have so long groaned under when ever they have a power

to do it? For no government can have a right to obedience from a people who have not freely consented to it: which they can never be supposed to do, till either they are put in a full state of liberty to choose their government and governors, or at least till they have such standing laws, to which they have by themselves or their representatives, given their free consent, and also till they are allowed their due property, which is so to be proprietors of what they have, that nobody can take away any part of it without their own consent, without which, men under any government are not in the state of freemen, but are direct slaves under the force of war.

193. But granting that the *conqueror* in a just war has a right to the estates, as well as power over the persons of the conquered; which, 'tis plain, he *hath* not: nothing of *absolute power* will follow from hence, in the continuance of the government. Because the descendants of these being all freemen, if he grants them estates and possessions to inhabit his country (without which it would be worth nothing) whatsoever he grants them, they have, so far as it is granted, *property* in. The nature whereof is, that *without a man's own consent* it *cannot be taken from him.*

194. Their *persons* are *free* by a native right, and their *properties,* be they more or less, are *their own, and at their own dispose,* and not at his; or else it is no property. Supposing the conqueror gives to one man a thousand acres, to him and his heirs for ever; to another he lets a thousand acres for his life, under the rent of £50 or £500 *per annum.* Has not the one of these a right to his thousand acres for ever, and the other, during his life, paying the said rent? And hath not the tenant for life a *property* in all that he gets over and above his rent, by his labour and industry during the said term, supposing it be double the rent? Can any one say, the king or conqueror, after his grant, may, by his power of conqueror, take away all, or part of the land from the heirs of one, or from the other, during his life, he paying the rent? Or can he take away from either, the goods or money they have got upon the said land, at his pleasure? If he can, then all free and voluntary contracts cease, and are void, in the world; there needs nothing to dissolve them at any time but power enough: and all the *grants* and promises *of men in power* are but mockery and

collusion. For can there be anything more ridiculous than to say, I give you and yours this for ever; and that in the surest and most solemn way of conveyance can be devised: and yet it is to be understood, that I have right, if I please, to take it away from you again to-morrow?

195. I will not dispute now whether princes are exempt from the laws of their country; but this I am sure, they owe subjection to the laws of God and nature. No body, no power can exempt them from the obligations of that eternal law. Those are so great, and so strong, in the case of *promises,* that Omnipotency itself can be tied by them. *Grants, promises,* and *oaths* are bonds that *hold the Almighty:* whatever some flatterers say to princes of the world who all together, with all their people joined to them, are, in comparison of the great God, but as a drop of the bucket, or a dust on the balance, inconsiderable nothing!

196. The short of the *case in conquest* is this. The conqueror, if he have a just cause, has a despotical right over the persons of all that actually aided, and concurred in the war against him, and a right to make up his damage and cost out of their labour and estates, so he injure not the right of any other. Over the rest of the people, if there were any that consented not to the war, and over the children of the captives themselves, or the possessions of either he has no power; and so can have, *by virtue of conquest, no lawful title* himself *to dominion* over them, or derive it to his posterity; but is an aggressor, if he attempts upon their properties and thereby puts himself in a state of war against them; and has no better a right of principality, he, nor any of his successors, than *Hingar,* or *Hubba,* the *Danes,*[3] had here in *England* or *Spartacus,*[4] had he conquered *Italy* would have had; which is to have their yoke cast off, as soon as God shall give those under their subjection courage and opportunity to do it. Thus, notwithstanding whatever title the kings of *Assyria* had over *Judah,* by the sword, God assisted *Hezekiah* to throw off the dominion of that conquering empire. *And the Lord was with*

[3]***Hingar. . .Danes:*** In the eighth and ninth centuries (A.D.) hordes of Northmen invaded other parts of Europe, including England.
[4]***Spartacus:*** Roman gladiator who led a slave revolt from 73–71 B.C.

Hezekiah, and he prospered; wherefore he went forth, and he rebelled against the king of Assyria, and served him not; 2 Kings 18. 7. Whence it is plain, that shaking off a power which force, and not right hath set over any one, though it hath the name of *rebellion,* yet is no offence before God, but is that which he allows and countenances, though even promises and covenants, when obtained by force, have intervened. For 'tis very probable to any one that reads the story of *Ahaz,* and *Hezekiah*[5] attentively, that the *Assyrians* subdued *Ahaz,* and deposed him, and made *Hezekiah* king in his father's lifetime; and that *Hezekiah,* by agreement, had done him homage, and paid him tribute all this time.

[5]***Ahaz . . . Hezekiah:*** see 2 *Kings:* 16–18.

XVII
Of Usurpation

197. As conquest may be called a foreign usurpation, so *usurpation* is a kind of domestic conquest, with this difference, that an usurper can never have right on his side, it being no *usurpation* but where one *is* got into *the possession of what another has right to.* This, so far as it is *usurpation,* is a change only of persons, but not of the forms and rules of the government: for if the usurper extend his power beyond, what of right belonged to the lawful princes, or governors of the commonwealth, 'tis *tyranny* added to usurpation.

198. In all lawful governments the designation of the persons, who are to bear rule, is as natural and necessary a part, as the form of the government it self, and is that which had its establishment originally from the people, the anarchy being much alike, to have no form of government at all; or to agree, that it shall be monarchical, but to appoint no way to design the person that shall have the power, and be the monarch. Hence all commonwealths with the form of government established, have rules also of appointing those, who are to have any share in the public authority; and settled methods of conveying the right to them. For the anarchy is much alike to have no form of government at all; or to agree that it shall be monarchical, but to appoint no way to know or design the person that shall have the power and be the monarch. Whoever gets into the exercise of any part of the power, by other ways, than what the laws of the community have prescribed, hath no right to be obeyed, though the form of the commonwealth be still preserved since he is not the person the laws have appointed, and consequently not the person the people have consented to. Nor can such an *usurper,* or any deriving from him, ever have a title, till the people are

both at liberty to consent, and have actually consented to allow, and confirm in him, the power he hath till then usurped.

XVIII
Of Tyranny

199. As usurpation is the exercise of power, which another hath a right to; so *tyranny is the exercise of power beyond right,* which no body can have a right to. And this is making use of the power any one has in his hands; not for the good of those, who are under it, but for his own private separate advantage. When the governor, however entitled, makes not the law, but his will, the rule; and his commands and actions are not directed to the preservation of the properties of his people, but the satisfaction of his own ambition, revenge, covetousness, or any other irregular passion.

200. If one can doubt this to be truth, or reason, because it comes from the obscure hand of a subject, I hope the authority of a king will make it pass with him. King *James the First,*[1] in his speech to the Parliament, 1603, tells them thus; *I will ever prefer the weal of the public, and of the whole commonwealth, in making of good laws and constitutions to any particular and private ends of mine. Thinking ever the wealth and weal of the commonwealth, to be my greatest weal, and worldly felicity; a point wherein a lawful king doth directly differ from a tyrant. For I do acknowledge, that the special and greatest point of difference that is between a rightful king, and an usurping tyrant, is this, That whereas the proud and ambitious tyrant doth think his kingdom and people are only ordained for satisfaction of his desires and unreasonable appetites; the righteous and just king doth by the contrary acknowledge himself to be*

[1]**King James I:** See C. H. McIlwain, *The Political Works of James I* (Cambridge, Mass.: Harvard University Press, 1918). Peter Laslett, in his edition of *Two Treatises,* notices that Locke appears to have altered the word "prosperitie" to read "property" in the text printed in the *Second Treatise* (see near the end of the first quoted passage).

ordained for the procuring of the wealth and property of his people. And again in his speech to the Parliament, 1609, he hath these words: *The KING binds himself by a double oath, to the observation of the fundamental laws of his kingdom. Tacitly, as by being a king, and so bound to protect as well the people as the laws of his kingdom, and expressly by his oath at his coronation; so as every just king, in a settled kingdom is bound to observe that paction made to his people by his laws in framing his government agreeable thereunto, according to that paction which God made with Noah, after the deluge: Hereafter, seedtime and harvest, and cold and heat, and summer and winter, and day and night shall not cease while the earth remaineth. And therefore a king governing in a settled kingdom, leaves to be a king, and degenerates into a tyrant as soon as he leaves off to rule according to his laws.* And a little after: *Therefore all kings that are not tyrants, or perjured, will be glad to bound themselves within the limits of their laws. And they that persuade them the contrary, are vipers, and pests both against them and the commonwealth.* Thus that learned king who well understood the notions of things, makes the difference betwixt a *king* and a *tyrant* to consist only in this, That one makes the laws the bounds of his power, and the good of the public, the end of his government; the other makes all give way to his own will and appetite.

201. 'Tis a mistake to think this fault is proper only to monarchies; other forms of government are liable to it, as well as that. For wherever the power that is put in any hands of the government of the people, and the preservation of their properties, is applied to other ends, and made use of to impoverish, harass, or subdue them to the arbitrary and irregular commands of those that have it: there it presently becomes *tyranny,* whether those that thus use it are one or many. Thus we read of the Thirty Tyrants at *Athens,* as well as one at *Syracuse;* and the intolerable dominion of the *Decemviri* at *Rome* was nothing better.[2]

[2]**Thirty Tyrants . . . *Rome:*** Thirty Tyrants is the name given to the oligarchic rulers of Athens, 404–3 B.C. They were led by cruel men such as Critias. Hiero became the tyrannical ruler of Syracuse in the third century A.D. (see Machiavelli, *The Prince,* Chapter 6). The *Decemviri* was the group of ten Patricians who were appointed in

202. *Wherever law ends, tyranny begins,* if the law be transgressed to another's harm. And whosoever in authority exceeds the power given him by the law, and makes use of the force he has under his command, to compass that upon the subject which the law allows not, ceases in that to be a magistrate, and acting without authority, may be opposed, as any other man, who by force invades the right of another. This is acknowledged in subordinate magistrates. He that hath authority to seize my person in the street, may be opposed as a thief and a robber, if he endeavours to break into my house to execute a writ, notwithstanding that I know he has such a warrant, and such a legal authority as will empower him to arrest me abroad. And why this should not hold in the highest, as well as in the most inferior magistrate, I would gladly be informed. Is it reasonable that the eldest brother, because he has the greatest part of his father's estate, should thereby have a right to take away any of his younger brother's portions? Or that a rich man, who possessed a whole country should from thence have a right to seize, when he pleased the cottage and garden of his poor neighbour? The being rightfully possessed of great power and riches exceedingly beyond the greatest part of the sons of *Adam,* is so far from being an excuse, much less a reason, for rapine, and oppression, which the endamaging another without authority is, that it is a great aggravation of it. For the exceeding the bounds of authority is no more a right in a great, than a petty officer; no more justifiable in a king than a constable. But is so much the worse in him, in that he has more trust put in him, has already a much greater share than the rest of his brethren, and is supposed from the advantages of education, employment and counsellors to be more knowing in the measures of right or wrong.

203. May the *commands* then *of a prince be opposed?* May he be resisted as often as any one shall find himself aggrieved, and but imagine he has not right done him? This will unhinge and overturn all polities, and instead of gov-

---

Rome to draw up a code of laws, and who for a time had supreme power. They were forced out in 449 B.C.

ernment and order, leave nothing but anarchy and confusion.

204. To this I answer: That *force* is to be *opposed* to nothing, but to unjust and unlawful *force;* whoever makes any opposition in any other case, draws on himself a just condemnation both from God and man; and so no such danger or confusion will follow, as is often suggested. For,

205. *First,* As in some countries, the person of the prince by the law is sacred; and so whatever he commands, or does, his person is still free from all question or violence, not liable to force, or any judicial censure or condemnation. But yet opposition may be made to the illegal acts of any inferior officer, or other commissioned by him; unless he will by actually putting himself into a state of war with his people, dissolve the government, and leave them to that defence, which belongs to every one in the state of nature. For of such things who can tell what the end will be? And a neighbour kingdom has showed the world an odd example. In all other cases the *sacredness* of the person *exempts him from all inconveniencies* whereby he is secure, whilst the government stands, from all violence and harm whatsoever; than which there cannot be a wiser constitution. For the harm he can do in his own person, not being likely to happen often, nor to extend itself far; nor being able by his single strength to subvert the laws, nor oppress the body of the people, should any prince have so much weakness and ill nature as to be willing to do it, the inconveniency of some particular mischiefs, that may happen sometimes, when a heady prince comes to the throne, are well recompensed by the peace of the public, and security of the government, in the person of the chief magistrate, thus set out of the reach of danger: It being safer for the body, that some few private men should be sometimes in danger to suffer, than that the head of the republic should be easily, and upon slight occasions exposed.

206. *Secondly,* But this privilege, belonging only to the king's person, hinders not, but they may be questioned, opposed, and resisted, who use unjust force, though they pretend a commission from him, which the law authorizes not. As is plain in the case of him, that has the king's writ to arrest a man, which is a full commission from the king; and yet he that has it cannot break open a man's house to

do it, nor execute this command of the king upon certain days, nor in certain places, though this commission have no such exception in it, but they are the limitations of the law, which if any one transgress, the king's commission excuses him not. For the king's authority being given him only by the law, he cannot empower any one to act against the law, or justify him, by his commission in so doing. The *commission* or *command of any magistrate, where he has no authority,* being as *void* and insignificant, as that of any private man. The difference between the one and the other, being that the magistrate has some authority so far, and to such ends, and the private man has none at all. For 'tis not the *commission,* but the *authority* that gives the right of acting; and *against the laws there can be no authority.* But, notwithstanding such resistance, the king's person and authority are still both secured, and so *no danger to governor or government.*

207. *Thirdly,* Supposing a government wherein the person of the chief magistrate is not thus sacred; yet this *doctrine* of the lawfulness of *resisting* all unlawful exercises of his power, *will not* upon every slight occasion endanger him, or *embroil the government.* For where the injured party may be relieved, and his damages repaired by appeal to the law, there can be no pretence for force, which is only to be used, where a man is intercepted from appealing to the law. For nothing is to be accounted hostile force, but where it leaves not the remedy of such an appeal. And 'tis such *force* alone, that *puts* him that uses it *into a state of war,* and makes it lawful to resist him. A man with a sword in his hand demands my purse in the highway, when perhaps I have not 12d. in my pocket; this man I may lawfully kill. To another I deliver £100 to hold only whilst I alight, which he refuses to restore me, when I am got up again, but draws his sword to defend the possession of it by force, if I endeavour to retake it. The mischief this man does me, is a hundred, or possibly a thousand times more, than the other perhaps intended me (whom I killed before he really did me any) and yet I might lawfully kill the one, and cannot so much as hurt the other lawfully. The reason whereof is plain; because the one using *force,* which threatened my life, I could not have *time* to appeal to the law to secure it: and when it was gone 'twas too late to appeal. The law could not restore life to my dead carcass: The loss was

irreparable; which to prevent, the law of nature gave me a right to *destroy* him, who had put himself into a state of war with me, and threatened my destruction. But in the other case, my life not being in danger, I might have the *benefit of appealing* to the law, and have reparation for my £100 that way.

208. *Fourthly,* But if the unlawful acts done by the magistrate, be maintained (by the power he has got) and the remedy which is due by law, be by the same power obstructed; yet the *right of resisting,* even in such manifest acts of tyranny, *will not* suddenly, or on slight occasions, *disturb the government.* For if it reach no farther than some private men's cases, though they have a right to defend themselves, and to recover by force, what by unlawful force is taken from them; yet the right to do so, will not easily engage them in a contest, wherein they are sure to perish; it being as impossible for one or a few oppressed men to *disturb the government,* where the body of the people do not think themselves concerned in it, as for a raving madman, or heady malcontent to overturn a well-settled state; the people being as little apt to follow the one, as the other.

209. But if either these illegal acts have extended to the majority of the people; or if the mischief and oppression has light only on some few, but in such cases, as the precedent, and consequences seem to threaten all, and they are persuaded in their consciences that their laws, and with them their estates, liberties, and lives are in danger, and perhaps their religion too, how they will be hindered from resisting illegal force used against them, I cannot tell. This is an *inconvenience,* I confess, that *attends all governments* whatsoever, when the governors have brought it to this pass, to be generally suspected of their people; the most dangerous state they can possibly put themselves in: wherein they are the less to be pitied, because it is so easy to be avoided; it being as impossible for a governor, if he really means the good of his people, and the preservation of them and their laws together, not to make them see and feel it; as it is for the father of a family, not to let his children see he loves, and takes care of them.

210. But if all the world shall observe pretences of one kind, and actions of another; arts used to elude the law, and the trust of prerogative (which is an arbitrary power in

some things left in the prince's hand to do good, not harm to the people) employed contrary to the end, for which it was given: if the people shall find the ministers, and subordinate magistrates chosen suitable to such ends, and favoured, or laid by proportionably, as they promote or oppose them: If they see several experiments made of arbitrary power, and that religion underhand favoured (though publicly proclaimed against) which is readiest to introduce it, and the operators in it supported, as much as may be; and when that cannot be done, yet approved still, and liked the better: if a *long train of actings show the councils* all tending that way, how can a man any more hinder himself from being persuaded in his own mind, which way things are going; or from casting about how to save himself, than he could from believing the captain of a ship he was in, was carrying him, and the rest of the company to *Algiers,*[3] when he found him always steering that course, though cross winds, leaks in his ship, and want of men and provisions did often force him to turn his course another way for some time, which he steadily returned to again as soon as the wind, weather, and other circumstances would let him?

[3]***Algiers:*** Part of the old Barbary Coast. Moslem pirates preyed on ships of Christian nations; and Christian captives sometimes were sold as slaves in the ports of the Barbary Coast.

XIX
Of the Dissolution of Government

211. He that will with any clearness speak of the *dissolution of government,* ought, in the first place to distinguish between the *dissolution of the society,* and the *dissolution of the government.* That which makes the community, and brings men out of the loose state of nature, into *one politic society,* is the agreement which every one has with the rest to incorporate, and act as one body, and so be one distinct commonwealth. The usual, and almost only way whereby *this union is dissolved,* is the inroad of foreign force making a conquest upon them. For in that case, (not being able to maintain and support themselves as one entire and *independent* body) the union belonging to that body which consisted therein, must necessarily cease, and so every one return to the state he was in before, with a liberty to shift for himself, and provide for his own safety as he thinks fit in some other society. Whenever the *society is dissolved,* 'tis certain the government of that society cannot remain. Thus conquerors' swords often cut up governments by the roots, and mangle societies to pieces, separating the subdued or scattered multitude from the protection of, and dependence on that society which ought to have preserved them from violence. The world is too well instructed in, and too forward to allow of this way of dissolving of governments to need any more to be said of it: and there wants not much argument to prove, that where the *society is dissolved,* the government cannot remain; that being as impossible, as for the frame of an house to subsist when the materials of it are scattered, and dissipated by a whirlwind, or jumbled into a confused heap by an earthquake.

212. Besides this overturning from without, *governments are dissolved from within,*

First, When the *legislative* is *altered.* Civil society being a state of peace, amongst those who are of it, from whom the state of war is excluded by the umpirage, which they have provided in their legislative, for the ending all differences, that may arise amongst any of them, 'tis in their *legislative,* that the members of a commonwealth are united, and combined together into one coherent living body. This *is the soul that gives form, life, and unity* to the commonwealth. From hence the several members have their mutual influence, sympathy, and connexion: And therefore when the *legislative* is broken, or *dissolved,* dissolution and death follows. For the *essence and union of the society* consisting in having one will, the legislative, when once established by the majority, has the declaring, and as it were keeping of that will. The *constitution of the legislative* is the first and fundamental act of society, whereby provision is made for the *continuation of their union,* under the direction of persons, and bonds of laws made by persons authorized thereunto, by the consent and appointment of the people, without which no one man, or number of men, amongst them, can have authority of making laws, that shall be binding to the rest. When any one, or more, shall take upon them to make laws, whom the people have not appointed so to do, they make laws without authority, which the people are not therefore bound to obey; by which means they come again to be out of subjection, and may constitute to themselves a *new legislative,* as they think best, being in full liberty to resist the force of those, who without authority would impose any thing upon them. Every one is at the disposure of his own will, when those who had by the delegation of the society, the declaring of the public will, are excluded from it, and others usurp the place who have no such authority or delegation.

213. This being usually brought about by such in the commonwealth who misuse the power they have: it is hard to consider it aright; and know at whose door to lay it, without knowing the form of government in which it happens. Let us suppose then the legislative placed in the concurrence of three distinct persons.

1. A single hereditary person having the constant, su-

preme, executive power, and with it the power of convoking and dissolving the other two within certain periods of time.

2. An assembly of hereditary nobility.

3. An assembly of representatives chosen *pro tempore,*[1] by the people: Such a form of government supposed, it is evident:

214. *First,* That when such a single person or prince sets up his own arbitrary will, in place of the laws, which are the will of the society, declared by the legislative, then the *legislative is changed.* For that being in effect the legislative whose rules and laws are put in execution, and required to be obeyed; when other laws are set up, and other rules pretended, and enforced, than what the legislative, constituted by the society, have enacted, 'tis plain, that the *legislative is changed.* Whoever introduces new laws, not being thereunto authorized by the fundamental appointment of the society, or subverts the old, disowns and overturns the power by which they were made, and so sets up a *new legislative.*

215. *Secondly,* When the prince hinders the legislative from assembling in its due time, or from acting freely, pursuant to those ends, for which it was constituted, the *legislative is altered.* For 'tis not a certain number of men, no, nor their meeting, unless they have also freedom of debating and leisure of perfecting, what is for the good of the society wherein the legislative consists: when these are taken away or altered, so as to deprive the society of the due exercise of their power, the *legislative* is truly *altered.* For 'tis not names, that constitute governments, but the use and exercise of those powers that were intended to accompany them; so that he who takes away the freedom, or hinders the acting of the legislative in its due seasons, in effect *takes away the legislative,* and *puts an end to the government.*

216. *Thirdly,* When by the arbitrary power of the prince, the electors, or ways of election are altered, without the consent, and contrary to the common interest of the people, there also the *legislative is altered.* For if others, than those whom the society hath authorized thereunto, do

[1]***pro tempore:*** "For a time," that is, elected for stated periods.

choose, or in another way, than what the society hath prescribed, those chosen are not the legislative appointed by the people.

217. *Fourthly,* The delivery also of the people into the subjection of a foreign power, either by the prince, or by the legislative, is certainly a *change of the legislative,* and so a *dissolution of the government.* For the end why people entered into society, being to be preserved one entire, free, independent society, to be governed by its own laws; this is lost, whenever they are given up into the power of another.

218. Why in such a constitution as this, the *dissolution of the government* in these cases is to be imputed to the prince, is evident: because he having the force, treasure, and offices of the state to employ, and often persuading himself, or being flattered by others, that as supreme magistrate he is uncapable of control; he alone is in a condition to make great advances toward such changes, under pretence of lawful authority, and has it in his hands to terrify or suppress opposers, as factious, seditious, and enemies to the government: whereas no other part of the legislative, or people is capable by themselves to attempt any alteration of the legislative, without open and visible rebellion, apt enough to be taken notice of; which when it prevails, produces effects very little different from foreign conquest. Besides the prince in such a form of government, having the power of dissolving the other parts of the legislative, and thereby rendering them private persons, they can never in opposition to him, or without his concurrence, alter the legislative by a law, his consent being necessary to give any of their decrees that sanction. But yet so far as the other parts of the legislative any way contribute to any attempt upon the government, and do either promote, or not, what lies in them, hinder such designs, they are guilty, and partake in this; which is certainly the greatest crime men can be guilty of one towards another.

219. There is one way more whereby such a government may be dissolved, and that is, when he who has the supreme executive power, neglects and abandons that charge, so that the laws already made can no longer be put in execution. This is demonstratively to reduce all to anarchy, and so effectively to *dissolve the government.* For

laws not being made for themselves, but to be by their execution the bonds of the society, to keep every part of the body politic in its due place and function, when that totally ceases, the *government* visibly *ceases,* and the people become a confused multitude, without order or connexion. Where there is no longer the administration of justice, for the securing of men's rights, nor any remaining power within the community to direct the force, or provide for the necessities of the public, there certainly is *no government left.* Where the laws cannot be executed, it is all one as if there were no laws, and a government without laws, is, I suppose, a mystery in politics, unconceivable to human capacity, and inconsistent with human society.

220. In these and the like cases, *when the government is dissolved,* the people are at liberty to provide for themselves, by erecting a new legislative, differing from the other, by the change of persons, or form, or both, as they shall find it most for their safety and good. For the society can never, by the fault of another, lose the native and original right it has to preserve itself, which can only be done by a settled legislative, and a fair and impartial execution of the laws made by it. But the state of mankind is not so miserable that they are not capable of using this remedy, till it be too late to look for any. To tell *people* they *may provide for themselves,* by erecting a new legislative, when by oppression, artifice, or being delivered over to a foreign power, their old one is gone, is only to tell them they may expect relief, when it is too late, and the evil is past cure. This is in effect no more than to bid them first be slaves, and then to take care of their liberty; and when their chains are on, tell them, they may act like freemen. This, if barely so, is rather mockery than relief; and men can never be secure from tyranny, if there be no means to escape it, till they are perfectly under it: And therefore it is, that they have not only a right to get out of it, but to prevent it.

221. There is therefore, Secondly, another way whereby *governments are dissolved,* and that is, when the legislative, or the prince either of them act contrary to their trust.

First, The *legislative acts against the trust* reposed in them, when they endeavour to invade the property of the subject, and to make themselves, or any part of the community, masters or arbitrary disposers of the lives, liberties, or fortunes of the people.

222. The reason why men enter into society, is the preservation of their property; and the end why they choose and authorize a legislative, is, that there may be laws made, and rules set as guards and fences to the properties of all the members of the society, to limit the power, and moderate the dominion of every part and member of the society. For since it can never be supposed to be the will of the society, that the legislative should have a power to destroy that, which every one designs to secure by entering into society, and for which the people submitted themselves to the legislators of their own making; whenever the *legislators endeavour to take away, and destroy the property of the people,* or to reduce them to slavery under arbitrary power, they put themselves into a state of war with the people, who are thereupon absolved from any farther obedience, and are left to the common refuge, which God hath provided for all men, against force and violence. Whensoever therefore the *legislative* shall transgress this fundamental rule of society; and either by ambition, fear, folly, or corruption, *endeavour to grasp* themselves, *or put into the hands of any other an absolute power* over the lives, liberties, and estates of the people; by this breach of trust they *forfeit the power,* the people had put into their hands, for quite contrary ends, and it devolves to the people, who have a right to resume their original liberty, and by the establishment of a new legislative (such as they shall think fit) provide for their own safety and security, which is the end for which they are in society. What I have said here, concerning the legislative in general, holds true also concerning the *supreme executor,* who having a double trust put in him, both to have a part in the legislative, and the supreme execution of the law, acts against both, when he goes about to set up his own arbitrary will, as the law of the society. He *acts* also *contrary to his trust* when he either employs the force, treasure, and offices of the society, to corrupt the *representatives* and gain them to his purposes: or openly pre-engages the *electors,* and prescribes to their choice, such, whom he has by solicitations, threats, promises, or otherwise won to his designs; and employs them to bring in such, who have promised

beforehand, what to vote, and what to enact. Thus to regulate candidates and *electors,* and new model the ways of *election,* what is it but to cut up the government by the roots, and poison the very fountain of public security? For the people having reserved to themselves the choice of their *representatives,* as the fence to their properties, could do it for no other end, but that they might always be freely chosen, and so chosen, freely act and advise, as the necessity of the commonwealth, and the public good should, upon examination, and mature debate, be judged to require. This, those who give their votes before they hear the debate, and have weighed the reasons on all sides, are not capable of doing. To prepare such an assembly as this, and endeavour to set up the declared abettors of his own will, for the true *representatives* of the people, and the law-makers of the society, is certainly as great a *breach of trust,* and as perfect a declaration of a design to subvert the government, as is possible to be met with. To which, if one shall add rewards and punishments visibly employed to the same end, and all the arts of perverted law made use of, to take off and destroy all that stand in the way of such a design, and will not comply and consent to betray the liberties of their country, 'twill be past doubt what is doing. What power they ought to have in the society, who thus employ it contrary to the trust went along with it in its first institution, is easy to determine; and one cannot but see, that he, who has once attempted any such thing as this, cannot any longer be trusted.

223. To this perhaps it will be said, that the people being ignorant, and always discontented, to lay the foundation of government in the unsteady opinion, and uncertain humour of the people, is to expose it to certain ruin; and *no government will be able long to subsist* if the people may set up a new legislative, whenever they take offence at the old one. To this I answer: Quite the contrary. People are not so easily got out of their old forms, as some are apt to suggest. They are hardly to be prevailed with to amend the acknowledged faults, in the frame they have been accustomed to. And if there be any original defects, or adventitious ones introduced by time, or corruption; 'tis not an easy thing to get them changed, even when all the world sees there is an opportunity for it. This slowness and aver-

sion in the people to quit their old constitutions, has, in the many revolutions[2] which have been seen in this kingdom, in this and former ages, still kept us to, or, after some interval of fruitless attempts, still brought us back again to our old legislative of king, lords and commons: and whatever provocations have made the crown be taken from some of our princes' heads, they never carried the people so far, as to place it in another line.

224. But 'twill be said, this *hypothesis* lays a *ferment* for frequent *rebellion.*[3] To which I answer:

First, No more than any other *hypothesis.* For when the *people* are made *miserable,* and find themselves *exposed to the ill usage of arbitrary power,* cry up their governors, as much as you will for sons of *Jupiter,* let them be sacred and divine, descended or authorized from Heaven; give them out for whom or what you please the same will happen. The *people generally ill treated,* and contrary to right, will be ready upon any occasion to ease themselves of a burden that sits heavy upon them. They will wish and seek for the opportunity, which, in the change, weakness, and accidents of humane affairs, seldom delays long to offer it self. He must have lived but a little while in the world, who has not seen examples of this in his time; and he must have read

[2]**revolutions:** Locke means great changes in the form of government—such as the forcible replacement of the monarchy with Cromwell's "Commonwealth," and then the restoration of the monarchy. But note that Locke never uses the phrase "right to revolution." Such a right, strictly speaking, is inconsistent with the end of government; for it implies that "the people" may rightly throw off even a well-constituted government.

[3]***rebellion:*** In this and the following sections, Locke carefully delineates what *he* means by "rebellion," and by "resistance." In section 226, he uses the word *rebellare,* which proves to be the Latin root of "rebellion." Locke pointedly observes that the meaning of the Latin is: "to bring *back* again the state of war" (emphasis supplied). He thus seeks to show that, contrary to the ordinary way of thinking, it is tyrannical rulers, not "the people," who are the true "rebels." Such rulers, by resorting to force, in opposition to the laws, make war on "the people" as surely as do foreign enemies. When this situation arises, "the people" have but two alternatives: to submit to plunder, torture, and execution; or to "resist." Locke unequivocal)y argues that resistance is the proper course.

very little, who cannot produce examples of it in all sorts of governments in the world.

225. Secondly, I answer, such *revolutions happen* not upon every little mismanagement in public affairs. *Great mistakes* in the ruling part, many wrong and inconvenient laws, and all the *slips* of human frailty will be *borne by the people* without mutiny or murmur. But if a long train of abuses, prevarications, and artifices, all tending the same way, make the design visible to the people, and they cannot but feel, what they lie under, and see, whither they are going; 'tis not to be wondered, that they should then rouse themselves, and endeavour to put the rule into such hands, which may secure to them the ends for which government was at first erected; and without which, ancient names, and specious forms, are so far from being better, that they are much worse, than the state of nature, or pure anarchy; the inconveniencies being all as great and as near, but the remedy farther off and more difficult.

226. Thirdly, I answer, That this doctrine of a power in the people of providing for their safety anew by a new legislative, when their legislators have acted contrary to their trust, by invading their property, is *the best fence against rebellion,* and the probablest means to hinder it. For rebellion being an opposition, not to persons, but authority, which is founded only in the constitutions and laws of the government; those, whoever they be, who by force break through, and by force justify their violation of them, are truly and properly *rebels.* For when men by entering into society and civil government, have excluded force, and introduced laws for the preservation of property, peace, and unity amongst themselves; those who set up force again in opposition to the laws, do *rebellare,* that is, bring back again the state of war, and are properly rebels: which they who are in power (by the pretence they have to authority, the temptation of force they have in their hands, and the flattery of those about them) being likeliest to do; the properest way to prevent the evil, is to show them the danger and injustice of it, who are under the greatest temptation to run into it.

227. In both the forementioned cases, when either the legislative is changed, or the legislators act contrary to the end for which they were constituted; those who are guilty

are *guilty of rebellion.* For if any one by force takes away the established legislative of any society, and the laws by them made pursuant to their trust, he thereby takes away the umpirage, which every one had consented to, for a peaceable decision of all their controversies, and a bar to the state of war amongst them. They, who remove, or change the legislative, take away this decisive power, which no body can have, but by the appointment and consent of the people; and so destroying the authority, which the people did, and no body else can set up, and introducing a power, which the people hath not authorized, they actually *introduce a state of war,* which is that of force without authority: and thus by removing the legislative established by the society (in whose decisions the people acquiesced and united, as to that of their own will) they untie the knot, and *expose the people anew to the state of war.* And if those, who by force take away the legislative, are *rebels,* the *legislators* themselves, as has been shown, can be no less esteemed so; when they, who were set up for the protection, and preservation of the people, their liberties and properties, shall by force invade, and endeavour to take them away; and so they putting themselves into a state of war with those, who made them the protectors and guardians of their peace, are properly, and with the greatest aggravation, *rebellantes* rebels.

228. But if they, who say it *lays a foundation for rebellion,* mean that it may occasion civil wars, or intestine broils, to tell the people they are absolved from obedience, when illegal attempts are made upon their liberties or properties, and may oppose the unlawful violence of those, who were their magistrates, when they invade their properties contrary to the trust put in them; and that therefore this doctrine is not to be allowed, being so destructive to the peace of the world. They may as well say upon the same ground, that honest men may not oppose robbers or pirates, because this may occasion disorder or bloodshed. If any *mischief* come in such cases, it is not *to be charged* upon him, who defends his own right, but *on him* that *invades* his neighbour's. If the innocent honest man must quietly quit all he has for peace sake, to him who will lay violent hands upon it, I desire it may be considered, what a kind of peace there will be in the world, which consists only in violence

and rapine; and which is to be maintained only for the benefit of robbers and oppressors. Who would not think it an admirable peace betwixt the mighty and the mean, when the lamb, without resistance, yielded his throat to be torn by the imperious wolf? *Polyphemus's*[4] den gives us a perfect pattern of such a peace, and such a government, wherein *Ulysses* and his companions had nothing to do, but quietly to suffer themselves to be devoured. And no doubt *Ulysses,* who was a prudent man, preached up *passive obedience,* and exhorted them to a quiet submission, by representing to them of what concernment peace was to mankind; and by showing the inconveniencies, might happen, if they should offer to resist *Polyphemus,* who had now the power over them.

229. The end of government is the good of mankind, and which is *best for mankind,* that the people should be always exposed to the boundless will of tyranny, or that the rulers should be sometimes liable to be opposed, when they grow exorbitant in the use of their power, and employ it for the destruction, and not the preservation of the properties of their people?

230. Nor let any one say, that mischief can arise from hence, as often as it shall please a busy head, or turbulent spirit, to desire the alteration of the government. 'Tis true, such men may stir whenever they please, but it will be only to their own just ruin and perdition. For till the mischief be grown general, and the ill designs of the rulers become visible, or their attempts sensible to the greater part, the people, who are more disposed to suffer, than right themselves by resistance, are not apt to stir. The examples of particular injustice, or oppression of here and there an unfortunate man, moves them not. But if they universally have a persuasion, grounded upon manifest evidence, that designs are carrying on against their liberties, and the general course and tendency of things cannot but give them strong suspicions of the evil intention of their governors, who is to be blamed for it? Who can help it, if they, who might avoid it, bring themselves into this suspicion? Are the people to be blamed, if they have the sense of rational

[4]***Polyphemus:*** One of the Cyclops Odysseus encounters. See *The Odyssey*, Book IX.

creatures, and can think of things no otherwise than as they find and feel them? And is it not rather *their fault,* who put things in such a posture that they would not have them thought, to be as they are? I grant that the pride, ambition, and turbulency of private men have sometimes caused great disorders in commonwealths, and factions have been fatal to states and kingdoms. But whether the *mischief* hath *oftener* begun *in the people's wantonness,* and a desire to cast off the lawful authority of their rulers; or *in the rulers' insolence,* and endeavours to get, and exercise an arbitrary power over their people; whether oppression, or disobedience gave the first rise to the disorder, I leave it to impartial history to determine. This I am sure, whoever, either ruler or subject, by force goes about to invade the rights of either prince or people, and lays the foundation for *overturning* the constitution and frame of *any just government,* is guilty of the greatest crime, I think, a man is capable of, being to answer for all those mischiefs of blood, rapine, and desolation, which the breaking to pieces of governments bring on a country, and he who does it, is justly to be esteemed the common enemy and pest of mankind; and is to be treated accordingly.

231. That *subjects* or *foreigners* attempting by force on the properties of any people, may be *resisted* with force, is agreed on all hands. But that *magistrates* doing the same thing, may be *resisted,* hath of late been denied: as if those who had the greatest privileges and advantages by the law, had thereby a power to break those laws, by which alone they were set in a better place than their brethren: whereas their offence is thereby the greater, both as being ungrateful for the greater share they have by the law, and breaking also that trust, whzch is put into their hands by their brethren.

232. Whosoever uses *force without right,* as every one does in society, who does it without law, puts himself into a state of war with those, against whom he so uses it, and in that state all former ties are cancelled, all other rights cease, and every one has a *right* to defend himself, and *to resist the aggressor.* This is so evident, that *Barclay*[5] himself,

[5] ***Barclay:*** William Barclay published two works (1600 and 1609) that defend the divine right of kings. Locke thus quotes from an "absolu-

that great assertor of the power and sacredness of kings, is forced to confess, that it is lawful for the people, in some cases, to resist their king; and that too in a chapter, wherein he pretends to show that the Divine law shuts up the people from all manner of rebellion. Whereby it is evident, even by his own doctrine, that, since they may in some cases resist, all resisting of *princes* is not rebellion. His words are these.

233. *But if any one should ask, Must the people then always lay themselves open to the cruelty and rage of tyranny? Must they see their cities pillaged, and laid in ashes, their wives and children exposed to the tyrant's lust and fury, and themselves and families reduced by their king, to ruin and all the miseries of want and oppression, and yet sit still? Must men alone be debarred the common privilege of opposing force with force, which nature allows so freely to all other creatures for their preservation from injury? I answer: Self-defence is a part of the law of nature; nor can it be denied the community, even against the king himself: but to revenge themselves upon him, must by no means be allowed them; it being not agreeable to that law. Wherefore if the king shall show an hatred, not only to some particular persons, but sets himself against the body of the commonwealth, whereof he is the head, and shall, with intolerable ill usage, cruelly tyrannize over the whole, or a considerable part of the people; in this case the people have a right to resist and defend themselves from injury: but it must be with this caution, that they only defend themselves, but do not attack their prince: They may repair the damages received, but must not for any provocation exceed the bounds of due reverence and respect. They may repulse the present attempt, but must not revenge past violences. For it is natural for us to defend life and limb, but that an inferior should punish a superior, is against nature. The mischief which is designed them, the people may prevent before it be done, but when it is done, they must not revenge it on the king, though author of the villany. This therefore is the*

---

tist," to show that even such men are compelled to admit *some* right of resistance, or else openly justify every tyranny, however terrible. In the original form of the *Two Treatises*, Locke first gives the Latin text, then an English translation. I have eliminated the Latin to save space. See Barclay's *De Regno . . . Monarchomachos*, 1600, Book III, Chapter 8.

privilege of the people in general, above what any private person hath; That particular men are allowed by our adversaries themselves to have no other remedy but patience; but the body of the people may with respect resist intolerable tyranny; for when it is but moderate, they ought to endure it.

234. Thus far that great advocate of monarchical power allows of *resistance.*

235. 'Tis true, he has annexed two limitations to it, to no purpose:

First. He says, it must be with reverence.

Secondly. It must be without retribution, or punishment; and the reason he gives, is, *Because an inferior cannot punish a superior.*

First, How to *resist force without striking again,* or how to *strike with reverence,* will need some skill to make intelligible. He that shall oppose an assault only with a shield to receive the blows, or in any more respectful posture, without a sword in his hand, to abate the confidence and force of the assailant, will quickly be at an end of his *resistance,* and will find such a defence serve only to draw on himself the worse usage. This is as ridiculous a way of *resisting* as *Juvenal*[6] thought it of fighting; *ubi tu pulsas, ego vapulo tantum.* And the success of the combat will be unavoidably the same he there describes it:

> *Libertas pauperis haec est:*
> *Pulsatus rogat, et pugnis concisus, adorat,*
> *Ut liceat paucis cum dentibus inde reverti.*

This will always be the event of such an imaginary *resistance,* where men may not strike again. He therefore *who may resist, must be allowed to strike.* And then let our author,

[6] ***Juvenal:*** Roman satirical poet (c. 60–140 A.D.). Locke quotes from *Satires,* III, 289–90; 299–301. The situation Juvenal describes is the encounter of a poor, honest citizen with a drunken bully on a dark street at night: "Whether you venture to say anything, or make off silently, it's all one: he will thrash you just the same, and then, in rage, take bail from you. Such is the liberty of the poor man: having been pounded and cuffed into a jelly, he begs and prays to be allowed to return home with a few teeth in his head." G. G. Ramsay, trans., *Juvenal and Persius* (Cambridge, Mass.: Harvard University Press, 1918).

or any body else join a knock on the head, or a cut on the face, with as much *reverence* and *respect* as he thinks fit. He that can reconcile blows and reverence, may, for aught I know, deserve for his pains, a civil respectful cudgelling wherever he can meet with it.

Secondly, As to his second, *An inferior cannot punish a superior;* that is true, generally speaking, whilst he is his superior. But to resist force with force, being *the state of war* that *levels the parties,* cancels all former relation of reverence, respect, and *superiority:* and then the odds that remains, is, that he, who opposes the unjust aggressor, has this superiority over him, that he has a right, when he prevails, to punish the offender, both for the breach of the peace, and all the evils that followed upon it. *Barclay* therefore, in another place, more coherently to himself, denies it to be lawful to *resist* a king in any case. But he there assigns two cases, whereby a king may unking himself. His words are,

236-237. *What then, Can there no case happen wherein the people may of right, and by their own authority help themselves, take arms, and set upon their king, imperiously domineering over them? None at all, whilst he remains a king.* Honour the king, *and* he that resists the power, resists the ordinance of God; *are Divine oracles that will never permit it. The people therefore can never come by a power over him, unless he does something that makes him cease to be a king. For then he divests himself of his crown and dignity, and returns to the state of a private man, and the people become free and superior; the power which they had in the* interregnum, *before they crowned him king, devolving to them again. But there are but few miscarriages which bring the matter to this state. After considering it well on all sides, I can find but two. Two cases there are, I say, whereby a king* ipso facto, *becomes no king; and loses all power and regal authority over his people; which are also taken notice of by* Winzerus.[7] *The first is, if he endeavour to overturn the government, that is, if he have a purpose and design to ruin the kingdom and commonwealth, as it is recorded of* Nero, *that he resolved to cut off the senate and*

[7]**Winzerus:** Peter Laslett, in his edition of the *Two Treatises*, notices that Locke has miscopied. In the original the reference is to Ninian Winzet (1518–92), a Catholic writer.

people of Rome, *lay the city waste with fire and sword, and then remove to some other place. And of* Caligula, *that he openly declared, that he would be no longer a head to the people or senate, and that he had it in his thoughts to cut off the worthiest men of both ranks, and then retire to* Alexandria: *and he wished that the people had but one neck that he might dispatch them all at a blow. Such designs as these, when any king harbours in his thoughts and seriously promotes, he immediately gives up all care and thought of the commonwealth; and consequently forfeits the power of governing his subjects, as a master does the dominion over his slaves whom he hath abandoned.*

238. *The other case is, When a king makes himself the dependent of another, and subjects his kingdom which his ancestors left him, and the people put free into his hands, to the dominion of another. For however perhaps it may not be his intention to prejudice the people; yet because he has hereby lost the principal part of regal dignity* viz., *to be next and immediately under God, supreme in his kingdom; and also because he betrayed or forced his people, whose liberty he ought to have carefully preserved, into the power and dominion of a foreign nation. By this as it were alienation of his kingdom, he himself loses the power he had in it before, without transferring any the least right to those on whom he would have bestowed it; and so by this act sets the people free, and leaves them at their [own] disposal. One example of this is to be found in the* Scotch *annals.* [Bk. III. ch. 16]

239. In these cases *Barclay* the great champion of absolute monarchy, is forced to allow, That a king may be *resisted*, and *ceases to be a king*. That is in short, not to multiply cases: in whatsoever he has *no authority*, there he is no king, and may be resisted: for *wheresoever the authority ceases, the king ceases too,* and becomes like other men who have no authority. And these two cases he instances in, differ little from those above mentioned, to be destructive to governments, only that he has omitted the principle from which his doctrine flows; and that is, The breach of trust, in not preserving the form of government agreed on, and in not intending the end of government it self, which is the public good and preservation of property. When a king has dethroned himself, and put himself in a state of war with his people, what shall hinder them from prosecuting him who is no king, as they would any other man, who has put himself into a state of war with them; *Barclay,* and those of his

opinion, would do well to tell us. This farther I desire may be taken notice of out of *Barclay,* that he says, *The mischief that is designed them, the people may prevent before it be done,* whereby he allows *resistance* when tyranny is but in design. *Such designs as these* (says he) *when any king harbours in his thoughts and seriously promotes, he immediately gives up all care and thought of the commonwealth;* so that according to him the neglect of the public good is to be taken as an evidence of *design,* or at least for a sufficient cause of *resistance.* And the reason of all he gives in these words, *because he betrayed or forced his people whose liberty he ought carefully to have preserved.* What he adds *into the power and dominion of a foreign nation,* signifies nothing, the fault and forefeiture lying in the loss of their *liberty* which he *ought to have preserved,* and not in any distinction of the persons to whose dominion they were subjected. The people's right is equally invaded, and their liberty lost, whether they are made slaves to any of their own, or a *foreign nation;* and in this lies the injury, and against this only have they the right of defence. And there are instances to be found in all countries, which show that 'tis not the change of nations in the persons of their governors, but the change of government, that gives the offence. *Bilson,*[8] a bishop of our Church, and a great stickler for the power and prerogative of princes, does, if I mistake not, in his treatise of *Christian Subjection,* acknowledge, that *princes may forfeit their power* and their title to the obedience of their subjects; and if there needed authority in a case where reason is so plain, I could send my reader to *Bracton,*[9] *Fortescue,*[10] and the author of the Mirror,[11] and others; writers that cannot be suspected to be ignorant of our government, or enemies to it. But I thought *Hooker* alone might be enough to satisfy those men, who relying on him for their ecclesiastical polity, are

[8]***Bilson:*** Thomas Bilson (1546–1616), Bishop of Winchester. He was a harsh critic of Catholicism.

[9]***Bracton:*** Henry de Bracton (?–1268). He wrote an early treatise on English law, *De Legibus et Consuetudinibus Angliae*.

[10]***Fortescue:*** Sir John Fortescue (c. 1394–1476). Author of a celebrated work on English law, *De Laudibus Legum Angliae*.

[11]**the author of the Mirror:** Locke appears to allude to a work on law written by Andrew Horn (?–1328).

by a strange fate carried to deny those principles upon which he builds it. Whether they are herein made the tools of cunninger workmen, to pull down their own fabric, they were best look. This I am sure, their civil policy is so new, so dangerous, and so destructive to both rulers and people, that as former ages never could bear the broaching of it; so it may be hoped those to come, redeemed from the impositions of those *Egyptian* under-taskmasters, will abhor the memory of such servile flatterers, who whilst it seemed to serve their turn, resolved all government into absolute tyranny, and would have all men born to, what their mean souls fitted them for, slavery.[12]

240. Here, 'tis like, the common question will be made, *Who shall be judge* whether the prince or legislative act contrary to their trust? This, perhaps, ill-affected and factious men may spread amongst the people, when the prince only makes use of his due prerogative. To this I reply, *The people shall be judge;* for who shall be *judge* whether his trustee or deputy acts well, and according to the trust reposed in him; but he who deputes him, and must, by having deputed him, have still a power to discard him when he fails in his trust? If this be reasonable in particular cases of private men, why should it be otherwise in that of the greatest moment; where the welfare of millions is concerned, and also where the evil, if not prevented, is greater, and the redress very difficult, dear, and dangerous?

241. But, farther, this question, *(Who shall be judge?)* cannot mean, that there is no judge at all. For where there is no judicature on earth to decide controversies amongst men, *God* in heaven is *judge:* He alone, 'tis true, is judge of the right. But *every man* is *judge* for himself, as in all other cases, so in this, whether another hath put himself into a state of war with him, and whether he should appeal to the supreme Judge, as *Jephtha* did.

242. If a controversy arise betwixt a prince and some of the people, in a matter where the law is silent, or doubtful, and the thing be of great consequence; I should think the

[12]All the references of this section are intended to strengthen Locke's argument by an appeal to English authority.

proper *umpire,* in such a case, should be the body of the *people.* For in such cases where the prince hath a trust reposed in him, and is dispensed from the common ordinary rules of the law; there, if any men find themselves aggrieved, and think the prince acts contrary to, or beyond that trust, who so proper to *judge* as the body of the *people,* (who, at first, lodged that trust in him) how far they meant it should extend? But if the prince, or whoever they be in the administration, decline that way of determination; the appeal then lies nowhere but to Heaven. Force between either persons, who have no known superior on earth, or which permits no appeal to a judge on earth, being properly a state of war, wherein the appeal lies only to Heaven, and in that state the injured party must *judge* for himself; when he will think fit to make use of that appeal, and put himself upon it.

243. To conclude, The *power that every individual gave the society,* when he entered into it, can never revert to the individuals again, as long as the society lasts, but will always remain in the community; because without this, there can be no community, no commonwealth, which is contrary to the original agreement: so also when the society hath placed the legislative in any assembly of men, to continue in them and their successors, with direction and authority for providing such successors, the *legislative can never revert to the people* whilst that government lasts: because having provided a legislative with power to continue for ever, they have given up their political power to the legislative, and cannot resume it. But if they have set limits to the duration of their legislative, and made this supreme power in any person, or assembly, only temporary: or else when by the miscarriages of those in authority, it is forfeited; upon the forfeiture of their rulers, or at the determination of the time set, *it reverts to the society,* and the people have a right to act as supreme, and continue the legislative in themselves, or erect a new form, or under the old form place it in new hands, as they think good.

bibliography

Editions

The only modern, critical edition of *Two Treatises of Government* is that prepared by Peter Laslett, published by Cambridge University Press (1967). It contains the full text, a lengthy introduction, many notes, a collation of the text, and a bibliography.

Biography

The most recent and useful biography is that by Maurice Cranston, *John Locke*. London: Longmans, Green and Co.: 1957.

Commentary

Only a handful of the numerous studies on Locke are cited here. Those tending to be critical of some of the views expressed in the Introduction and notes to this edition are marked with an *.

Cox, Richard H. *Locke on War and Peace.* Oxford: At the Clarendon Press, 1960; "Justice as the Basis of Political Order in Locke." In *Justice,* edited by C. J. Friedrich and J. W. Chapman. New York: Atherton Press, 1963.

*Dunn, John. *The Political Thought of John Locke.* Cambridge, England: Cambridge University Press, 1968.

Goldwin, Robert. "John Locke." In *History of Political Philosophy,* 2d ed., edited by L. Strauss and J. Cropsey. Chicago: Rand McNally 1972.

Gough, J. W. *John Locke's Political Philosophy.* Oxford: At the Clarendon Press, 1950.

Kendall, Willmore. *John Locke and the Doctrine of Majority-Rule.* Urbana, Ill.: University of Illinois Press, 1941.

*Macpherson, C. B. "Locke: The political theory of appropriation." *The Political Theory of Possessive Individualism.* Oxford: At the Clarendon Press, 1962.

Mansfield, Harvey C., Jr. "On the Political Character of Property in Locke." In *Powers, Possessions, and Freedom: Essays in Honor of C. B. Macpherson,* edited by A. Kontos, pp. 23–38. Toronto: University of Toronto Press, 1979.

Strauss, Leo. *Natural Right and History* (Chapter V.B). Chicago: University of Chicago Press, 1953.

*Yolton, John, ed. *John Locke—Problems and Perspectives.* Cambridge, England: Cambridge University Press, 1968. Thirteen essays by different authors.